The Life-Changing Power of Jesus

Dr. David R. Reagan

www.lamblion.com
McKinney, Texas

Dedicated to the Memory of

Carl Ketcherside

whom the Lord used mightily in
the process of my sanctification.

First edition, 2024

ISBN: 978-0-945593-43-0

Library of Congress Control Number: 2024915586

Lamb & Lion Ministries
P.O. Box 919
McKinney, Texas 75070
lamblion@lamblion.com
www.lamblion.com

Cover design by Jana Olivieri and Adam Jordan.

Printed in the United States of America.

Contents

Books by Dr. David R. Reagan

The Christ in Prophecy Study Guide (1987, 2001 & 2006).

Trusting God: Learning to Walk by Faith (1987, 1994 & 2015).

Jesus is Coming Again! (1992 & 2015).

The Master Plan: Making Sense of the Controversies Surrounding Bible Prophecy Today (1993).

The Parched Soul of America: A Poet's View of Our National Decay (1994). Written with Kay Hedger.

Living for Christ in the End Times (2000 & 2015).

Wrath and Glory: Unveiling the Majestic Book of Revelation, (2001, 2016 & 2021).

America the Beautiful? The United States in Bible Prophecy (2003, 2006 & 2009).

God's Plan for the Ages: The Blueprint of Bible Prophecy (2005 & 2020).

Eternity: Heaven or Hell? (2010).

Jesus: The Lamb and The Lion (2011).

The Man of Lawlessness: The Antichrist in the Tribulation (2012).

A Prophetic Manifesto (2012 & 2018).

Living on Borrowed Time: the Imminent Return of Jesus (2013).

The Jewish People: Rejected or Beloved? (2014).

God's Prophetic Voices to America (2017 & 2018).

Israel in Bible Prophecy: Past, Present & Future (2017).

The Basics of Bible Prophecy (2018) Written with Darryl Nunnelley.

The Rapture: Fact or Fiction? (2019).

America's Suicide (2021).

What's the Difference in a Millennium and a Millipede? (2022).

Islam & Christianity: Roads to the Same God? (2022) Written together with Marko Kiroglu, Nathan Jones and Col. Tim Moore.

The 9 Wars of the End Times (2023).

How to Die With a Smile on Your Face (2023)

Amazing Grace

John Newton (1725-1807)

1) Amazing grace (how sweet the sound)
that saved a wretch like me!
I once was lost, but now am found,
was blind, but now I see.

2) 'Twas grace that taught my heart to fear,
and grace my fears relieved;
how precious did that grace appear
the hour I first believed!

3) Through many dangers, toils and snares
I have already come:
'tis grace has brought me safe thus far,
and grace will lead me home.

4) When we've been there ten thousand years,
Bright shining as the sun,
We've no less days to sing God's praise
Than when we first begun.

This great hymn was written by John Newton in 1772 and was sung for the first time at a worship service at his church on January 1, 1773. There is no evidence that Newton or any of his contemporaries ever felt the song was of any special quality. It appeared in contemporary hymn books with "the uninspiring title" of "Faith's Review and Expectation." It never caught on with churchgoers in England.

The hymn became popular for the first time in the United States during the 1830s. But this occurred only after it was given a new title, and the tune was changed to one rooted in Negro spirituals. Also, the fourth and fifth stanzas were dropped and a whole new stanza was added at the end by Edwin Othello Excell (1851-1921). The song has since become "the spiritual national anthem of America."

[Notes from *John Newton* by Jonathan Aitken, 2007, pages 226-237.]

Foreword

The Apostle Paul declared in Romans 1:16, "For I am not ashamed of the Gospel, because it is the power of God that brings salvation to everyone who believes, first to the Jew, then to the Gentiles."As you will read in this book, Paul knew firsthand the life-changing power of Jesus because his life had been dramatically transformed by the Savior.

Paul had also witnessed Jesus radically change the lives of thousands of others as the "good news" of Christ was shared and proclaimed. So Paul had complete and total confidence that anyone who would place their trust in Jesus would be forgiven of their sins. They would also be given a relationship with God, eternal life and the indwelling of the Holy Spirit to set them free from sin and change their life here on earth right now.

In this wonderful and encouraging book, Dr. David Reagan, gives overwhelming evidence of the life-changing power of Jesus by sharing with us the stories of twenty-two people whose lives were profoundly changed when they placed their faith in Jesus.

Three of these transformed lives are taken from the pages of the New Testament. Five of these amazing stories are about the lives of well-known people from history and how Jesus remarkably changed them. The final fourteen illustrations of Jesus' life-changing power are examples of men and women Dr. Reagan has known personally who all unashamedly declare like Paul, that Jesus miraculously changed their lives.

As you read each of these incredible stories of Jesus'

love, grace and saving power, your faith that Jesus can profoundly change your life and the lives of your family and friends will be greatly strengthened. You will be encouraged to pray confidently for those you love who need Jesus to save and transform them. You will gain an increased boldness in sharing this wonderful Gospel of Jesus, as you reflect on the testimonies of these men and women whose lives were delivered from the bondage of sin to become brand new people in Christ Jesus.

The last of these inspiring stories is that of Dr. Reagan himself. He too has been transformed by the life-changing power of Jesus. For over ten years I have had a front row seat to witness the life of this humble servant of God. As Dave's pastor, I have been the recipient of countless encouraging emails and words of support from him over these years.

Each week, unless he is preaching elsewhere, Brother Dave is sitting in the worship service, taking notes, attending multiple Bible Studies at our church and ministering to members of our church family. While leading an international ministry, writing books, producing weekly television programs and preaching all over the country, he has still demonstrated weekly, through his Christ-like service in our local church, the life-changing power of Jesus.

I know you are going to be blessed by these inspiring stories. Each of these lives are a trophy of God's grace and a demonstration of His incredible power and willingness to save and transform. No wonder we are not ashamed of the Gospel of Christ.

All glory to Jesus!

Glenn Meredith
Senior Pastor
Brookhaven Church, McKinney, Texas

Preface

I grew up believing that God retired at the end of the First Century, after the death of the last Apostle, John.

I was taught that at that point in history, all aspects of the supernatural ceased. Gifts of the Spirit were no longer given. Miracles were no longer a possibility. We were left to cope with life's problems and challenges with our common sense and the counsel provided by the Bible.

Our preachers mocked Pentecostals as ignorant, emotional and superstitious people who had deceived themselves into believing that God was still active in human affairs — giving direction and counsel and performing miracles.

A Troubling Memory

My most vivid memory of these beliefs was a full-page newspaper advertisement that was run in the *Ft. Worth Star Telegram* sometime in the 1960s. The big, bold headline of the ad read: "GOD DOES NOT HEAL!" The ad proceeded to claim that God had not healed anyone in the past 2,000 years. It was sponsored by a long list of churches affiliated with the denomination I grew up in — the Non-Instrumental Churches of Christ.

To emphasize their point, this group of churches offered a prize of $10,000 to any person who could prove that they had been miraculously healed.

The evening of the day the ad appeared, it was featured on one of the local Ft. Worth television news programs. They interviewed a disfigured Pentecostal pastor who claimed he was born deaf and blind and that he had been miraculously healed at a tent meeting through the laying on of hands and prayer. When asked if he had proof, he said he had lots of medical records from doctors who had examined him before and after his healing. He added that he could also provide many witnesses to his healing.

He was then asked if he was going to apply for the $10,000 reward. He laughed and said, "No!" When asked why, he replied, "Because it would be a waste of time. You see, I could present the preachers of these churches with stacks of medical documents, and they still would not believe."

A Similar Biblical Example

His answer reminded me of the time when Jesus told the story of a rich man and a poor one who both died and whose souls went to Hades, the poor man to a compartment called Paradise and the rich man to a compartment called Torments. The man in torment saw Abraham on the Paradise side of Hades and called out to him, "Father Abraham, have mercy on me." He then requested that he be allowed to go back and warn his five brothers of the place of torment that he was in.

Abraham answered that they did not need his warning because they had the writings of Moses and the Prophets. The rich man replied, "but if someone goes to them from the dead, they will repent." Abraham replied, " If they do not listen to Moses and Prophets, neither will they be persuaded if someone rises from the dead" (Luke 16:19-31).

These words proved to be prophetic, because later, when Jesus raised Lazarus from the dead after he had been in the tomb for four days, the chief priests and Pharisees began to plot the murder of Jesus (John 11:47 & 57).

When people are caught up in religion rather than a personal relationship with the Lord, they develop hardened hearts, and they will reject any evidence, no matter how dramatic or conclusive.

Biblical Principles Discovered

That newspaper advertisement and the subsequent TV interview provoked me to think seriously about the miraculous. I began an in-depth Bible study, and it did not take me long to come to three conclusions:

1) Most miracles are miracles of timing. One of many biblical examples I could cite is the story of Hannah which is recorded in 1 Samuel 1:1-20. Hannah was one of two wives that her husband had. The other wife had given birth to several children, but "Yahweh had closed Hannah's womb." Hannah was taunted constantly by the other wife until one day, Hannah turned to the Lord in prayer. She cried out fervently for God to bless her womb, and she promised that if He were to do so, she would dedicate the baby to lifetime service for the Lord. Yahweh did bless her womb, and she gave birth to a boy who was to become one of the greatest judges of Israel — Samuel. His birth did not contradict any laws of nature. Hannah had a husband. But the Bible presents it as a miracle — and it was a miracle of timing.

2) We can limit God's miracle working power by our unbelief. This happened to Jesus in His home town of Nazareth. We are told that He could perform only a few miracles there because of their unbelief (Mark 6:1-6).

3) God's greatest continuing daily miracle is the salvation of souls. Every second of every day throughout the world God, starts a total transformation in the lives of people when they place their faith in Jesus as their Lord and Savior. We find this transformation mentioned in the words of the Apostle John in 1 John 1:9 where he said, "If we confess our sins, He is faithful and just and will forgive us our sins and purify us from all unrighteousness."

A Personal Transformation

My discovery of these principles enabled me to take God out of the box I had put Him in. When I did that, my eyes were opened to the reality that He was performing miracles daily around me — the most significant being human transformations that were often so radical that they were almost unbelievable.

Those transformations are what this book is all about. As you read the examples given in this book, if you are not a Christian, I pray you will put your trust in Jesus as your Lord and Savior and open up yourself to a transformation that will bring you joy (Romans 15:13) and "the peace that passes all understanding" (Philippians 4:7).

Christianity is not just a religion for the future. It is a personal relationship with Jesus that will give meaning to your life here and now.

Hallelujah!

Dave Reagan
Allen, Texas
Summer of 2024

Introduction

God is in the Change Business

"Therefore if anyone is in Christ, he is a new creation; the old things have passed away; behold, new things have come."
(2 Corinthians 5:17)

The church I was born into and grew up in had God in a box. By this I mean that they had a long list of things which they declared God could no longer do.

Such a restrained view of God was due to a doctrine my church taught called "Cessationism." According to this doctrine — as I was taught it — all aspects of the supernatural ceased in the First Century at the death of the last apostle. Gifts of the Spirit ceased, and God no longer intervened in history by performing miracles. In short, the Holy Spirit retired, and we were left to cope with life by relying on common sense and God's Word.

We, in effect, became Deists, believing in an impersonal God.

Accordingly, we tended to think of salvation as simply a fire insurance policy whose greatest benefit was to keep us out of Hell!

Well, it is true that if you give your heart to Jesus, reaching out to Him in faith to receive Him as your Lord and Savior, one of the benefits will be a guarantee that you will never go to Hell. But the blessings of Christianity are far greater than just that, and those benefits apply to the here and now.

The Flaw of Cessationism

I think I should point out that there is a form of Cessationism that is less radical than what I was taught. This milder form takes the position that only the "miracle gifts" of tongues and healing have ceased. This group believes God can still perform miracles today, but the Holy Spirit no longer uses individuals to perform miracle signs.

I strongly disagree with this "milder" form of Cessationism. To me, it still puts God in a box. I believe the God of the Bible is still the God of today. And I know from personal experience that He often works through individuals to perform miracles.

For example, even though the ministry I established in 1980 is one that emphasizes the teaching of Bible prophecy, about two years after I formed it, I was given the gift of praying for barren wombs. Over the years, I have accumulated many photos of babies born to women who had been told by doctors that they could not conceive.

The basic problem with all forms of Cessationism is that they do not line up with what the Bible teaches. For example, the Apostle Paul in 1 Corinthians 1:7 stated that Christians would not be "lacking any gift" as they are "eagerly awaiting the revelation of our Lord Jesus Christ." That's a reference to the Lord's Second Coming. We are still awaiting that event, and so all the supernatural gifts of the Spirit must still be available.

Further, the Bible clearly teaches the immutability of God. That means that one of the basic characteristics of our Creator is that He never changes. Consider these key verses:

- Psalm 102:25-27 — "Of old You founded the earth, and the heavens are the work of Your hands. Even they will perish, but You will remain; and all of them will wear out like a garment; like clothing You will change them and they will be changed. But You are the same . . ."

- Malachi 3:6 — "For I, Yahweh, do not change . . ."
- Hebrews 13:8 — "Jesus Christ is the same yesterday and today and forever."

The True Personal and Powerful God of Today

As these verses clearly indicate, it is a matter of fact that the God of the Bible is still the God of today.

He is not an aloof and impersonal God like Allah, the false god of Islam. Instead, He continues to be a very personal God who is concerned about every aspect of our lives. And thus, we are told in 1 Peter 5:6-7 that we are to "humble yourselves under the mighty hand of God, that He may exalt you at the proper time, casting all your anxiety on Him, ***because He cares for you***" (emphasis added).

This very comforting Scripture passage is an echo of Isaiah 42:6 which reads: "I am Yahweh, I have called You in righteousness; I will also take hold of You by the hand and guard You . . ."

Consider also:

- Psalm 32:8 — "I will give you insight and teach you in the way which you should go; I will counsel you with My eye upon you."
- Psalm 103:13 — "As a father has compassion on his children, so Yahweh has compassion on those who fear Him."
- Psalm 139:3 — "You scrutinize my path and my lying down, and are intimately

acquainted with all my ways."

The personal, intense concern of God expressed in these Old Testament verses is repeated throughout the New Testament. For example, in Jesus' Sermon on the Mount, He warned strongly against Believers being worried or anxious about the necessities of life — like food, clothing and housing. He pointed out that if God is concerned about feeding the birds of the air, how much more so does He care about humans who have put their faith in Him. As recorded in Matthew 6, He asserted:

> 31) Do not worry then, saying, "What will we eat?" or "What will we drink?" or "What will we wear for clothing?"
>
> 32) For all these things the Gentiles eagerly seek; for your heavenly Father knows that you need all these things.
>
> 33) But seek first His kingdom and His righteousness, and all these things will be added to you.

The Apostle John reported that Jesus called Believers the "friends" of God (John 15:15). James, the brother of Jesus, told the First Century church , "Draw near to God and He will draw near to you." James added, "Humble yourselves in the presence of the Lord, and He will exalt you" (James 4:10).

These comments are not pointing to an aloof and disinterested God, for which we can shout, "Hallelujah!"

The fact that our Creator is a very personal God is the reason that the Apostle Paul could write these words in Philippians 4:

> 4) Rejoice in the Lord always; again I will say, rejoice!
>
> 5) Let your considerate spirit be known to all

men. The Lord is near.

6) Be anxious for nothing, but in everything by prayer and petition with thanksgiving let your requests be made known to God.

7) And the peace of God, which surpasses all comprehension, will guard your hearts and your minds in Christ Jesus.

Summary

God is still on His throne. He still hears prayers, and He still answers prayers. He still performs miracles.

And His greatest continuing miracle, which He performs every second all over the world, is the total transformation of people who receive His Son as their Lord and Savior.

He takes people who are wallowing in sin and debauchery, forgives their sins and starts cleansing them from the inside out through the power of His Holy Spirit, transforming them into the image of His Son.

The Nature of Salvation

Salvation is not just a one time event. It is a process. It consists of three stages, phases or facets.

It begins with **Justification**, which occurs the moment you put your faith in Jesus. This is the event that renders the Believer free from the penalty of sin.

Justification is a judicial concept. To be justified means that you stand before the judgment seat of God with all your sins forgiven and forgotten. They are forgiven because the righteousness of Jesus has been imputed to you. They are forgotten in the sense that they will never be held against you in the future.

Justification also means that your **spirit** which has been dead in sin is regenerated, and it begins to commune with the

Spirit of God.

Justification is by "grace through faith" (Ephesians 2:8-10). It is not something you can earn through good works. It seals you for Heaven (Romans 5:8-9).

The second step in salvation is **Sanctification** which relates to the **soul**. The soul consists of your mind, emotions and will.

When you are justified, you receive the gift of the in-dwelling presence of the Holy Spirit who goes to work on your feelings, attitudes and behavior — encouraging you where your conform to God's Word and convicting you in those areas where you fall short. This is a life-long process.

Justification determines your eternal destiny. Sanctification determines the degree to which you will live in the joy of the Lord here and now.

The goal of sanctification is to shape you more fully into the image of Jesus (Romans 8:29). Paul put it this way in 2 Corinthians 3:18 — "But we all, with unveiled face, beholding as in a mirror the glory of the Lord, are being transformed into the same image from glory to glory, just as from the Lord, the Spirit."

Whereas justification delivers Believers from the penalty of sin, sanctification frees us from the power of sin "because greater is He [the Holy Spirit] who is in you than he [Satan] who is in the world." (1 John 4:4).

When the Lord returns, our bodies will be resurrected and glorified, meaning they will be perfected and made immortal (Romans 8:23 & 30). **Glorification** completes the salvation process because at that point we are saved, body, soul and spirit.

Sanctification in the Bible

The sanctification process is mentioned in Romans 6:22,

where the Apostle Paul says:

> Having been freed from sin [justification] and enslaved to God, you derive your benefit, resulting in sanctification, and the outcome, eternal life [glorification].

Again, in 2 Thessalonians 2:13-14:

> God has chosen you from the beginning for salvation [justification] through sanctification by the Spirit . . . that you may gain the glory of our Lord Jesus Christ [glorification].

The Speed of Sanctification

The speed of the sanctification process varies per person, depending on attitudes. That's because the Bible says we can "quench" (1 Thessalonians 5:19), "grieve" (Ephesians 4:30) and even "blaspheme the Spirit" (Luke 12:10).

We quench the Spirit when we refuse to allow the Spirit to sit on the throne of our life. This usually results from a failure to abide in God's Word and thus to do what it says. This means it is possible for Christians to remain babes in Christ despite the fact that the Holy Spirit resides inside of them (1 Corinthians 3:2-3).

A Personal Experience

I learned a lesson from personal experience about the speed of sanctification many years ago when, at the age of 40, I had lunch with a man I had recently met who was 70 years old.

As we got acquainted, it quickly became apparent to me that I was talking with a spiritual giant. I finally asked him how long he had been a Christian, expecting him to say at least 50 years.

I was shocked when he said he had been what he called "a

true Christian" for only 10 years!

I asked him how that could be since he was so spiritually mature. I told him I had been a Christian for 30 years, and I was nowhere as spiritually mature as him.

"Well," he said, "I grew up in a church where you could believe anything you pleased. And despite the fact that I went to church all my life, I didn't become a born-again Christian until 10 years ago." Then, he added, "When the Jesus bus came by, I jumped on with enthusiasm and took off."

"But," he continued, "based on what you've told me about yourself, you attended a very legalistic church for 30 years that had a rigid doctrine for everything. Thus, when the Jesus bus finally came by for you, you failed to jump on because you had piles of doctrinal baggage you had accumulated, and while you stood there trying to decide what bags to take with you, the bus left. And that occurred over and over again until you decided to jettison the baggage, jump on the bus and fall in love with Jesus."

This insightful man really nailed me with that observation! It was exactly what had happened to me.

Another Sanctification Experience

Yes, because I grew up in a very doctrinally rigid church, my sanctification was curtailed by legalism. I was taught that my salvation depended upon my being right about every possible doctrine. In short, my church taught salvation by perfected knowledge.

I thus had an attitude toward those who differed from me that was very judgmental and condemnatory. Needless to say, this attitude seriously curtailed the work of the Holy Spirit in shaping me into the image of Jesus.

The man God used to deliver me from legalism is the man this book is dedicated to — namely, Carl Ketcherside (1908-

1989). Early in his life, Carl became well known as the champion debater of a hyper-legalistic sect within the Churches of Christ called, "The Anti's." Basically, this group was opposed to located ministers, missionary societies, orphan homes, musical instruments and many other items too numerous to name.

Carl Ketcherside

In 1951, while preaching in Belfast, Ireland, Carl had a profound spiritual experience that resulted in a radical transformation in his attitude. At the age of 43, he did something he had never done before — he asked Jesus into his heart. He was instantly delivered from religion to a personal relationship with Jesus. He returned to the States a new man, preaching the love of Jesus rather than the hatred of legalism.

Ketcherside's new message had a profound impact on me. Specifically, he taught me that "all truth is important; but all truth is not equally important." Thus, whatever may be the truth about the frequency of communion or the use of instrumental music or the mode of baptism, those truths are nothing compared to *The Truth* that Jesus is Lord. I was delivered from legalism, and my sanctification shifted out of idle into high gear!

Sanctification's Relation to Your Eternal Destiny

I want to emphasize once again that your sanctification is not related to your eternal destiny. Whether you end up in Heaven or Hell depends on your justification. Sanctification relates to your life in Christ here and now.

The reason sanctification is so important is because when we are justified by grace through faith in Jesus, we continue to dwell in a mortal body that has a sin nature. The Holy Spirit takes up residence in our bodies to assist us in spiritual warfare as we are confronted with temptations.

You can be certain that new Believers will be confronted because Satan will be enraged over their new faith. And since the Holy Spirit will be fighting for them, they will become aware of intense internal spiritual struggles like they have never experienced before.

The Apostle Paul spoke about this internal spiritual warfare in Romans 7. He began by admitting that even though he stood justified before God and was thus forgiven of his sins, he was still "fleshly" (verse 14). Because of that, he stated, "the willing [to follow God] is present in me, but the working out of the good is not. For the good that I want, I do not do, but I practice the very evil that I do not want" (verses 18-19).

At that point he cried out in despair, "Wretched man that I am! Who will deliver me from the body of this death?" (verse 24). He then quickly answered his own question with a glorious declaration: "There is now no condemnation for those who are in Christ Jesus. For the law of the Spirit of life in Christ Jesus has set you free from the law of sin and of death." (Romans 8:1-2). He continued in chapter 8 to explain that the key to victory over these internal spiritual struggles is to stay focused on Jesus and the working of His Spirit within us: "For the mind set on the flesh is death, but the mind set on the Spirit is life and peace. . ." (Romans 8:6).

There is another reason the internal spiritual battle intensifies after justification. It's due to the fact that when the Holy Spirit takes up residence in the new Believer, He starts identifying areas of the person's life that are out of alignment with God's Word. Sins that have never bothered us before suddenly make us miserable.

God is anxious to bring the lives of Believers into conformity with His Word so that they can experience the fullness of life in the Spirit. That's what sanctification is all about.

What's Coming

In the chapters to follow, I am going to give you many examples of the life-changing power of Jesus through justification and sanctification. I will begin with examples from the Scriptures. Next we will take a look at historical examples outside the Bible. I will conclude with first-hand examples from people I have known personally.

Wonderful Grace of Jesus

Haldor Lillenas (1885-1959)

(1918)

Wonderful Grace of Jesus,
Greater than all my sin;
How shall my tongue describe it,
Where shall its praise begin?
Taking away my burden,
Setting my spirit free;
O the Wonderful Grace of Jesus reaches me!

Refrain:
Wonderful the matchless Grace of Jesus,
Deeper than the mighty rolling sea;
Higher than the mountain, sparkling like a fountain,
All sufficient Grace for even me.
Broader than the scope of my transgressions,
Greater far than all my sin and shame.
O magnify the precious name of Jesus,
Praise His Name!

Biblical Examples

Chapter 1

A Zealous Pharisee

> "And I was advancing in Judaism beyond many of my contemporaries among my countrymen, being far more zealous for the traditions of my fathers."
>
> (Galatians 1:14)

I find it ironic that the most hateful and zealous persecutor of Christians in the birthing years of the Church turned out to be the greatest promoter of the Church and its message. I'm speaking, of course, of the person who came to be known as the Apostle Paul.

He was born in a Roman city called Tarsus, located in the Roman province of Cilicia. This province was located in the southern area of what is known today as the nation of Turkey, near the coast of the Mediterranean Sea and the place where Turkey intersects with Syria. (See the map on the next page.)

The Consummate Jew

He was born a Jew and was given the Hebrew name of Saul. He is known to most Christians today as the Apostle Paul. His name was not changed, as was the case with many Bible characters. Paul was simply the Greek version of his Hebrew name.

Because he was born in a Roman city, he was considered to be a Roman citizen from birth. This fact gave him a legal standing that would prove very valuable to him later in life when it protected him from violent treatment by the Roman authorities (Acts 22:22-29).

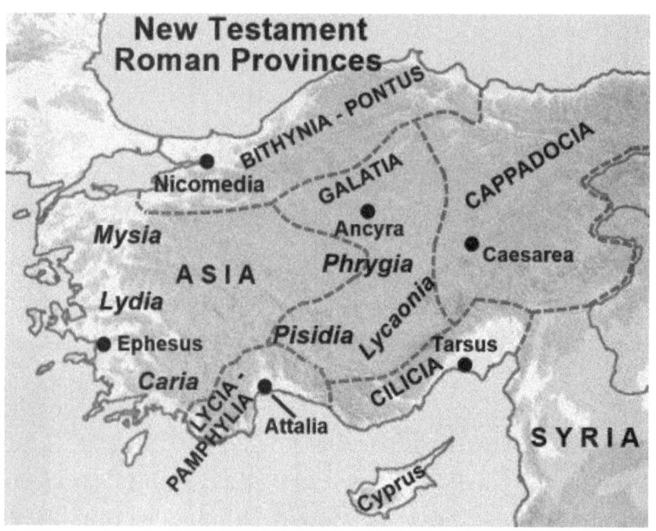

(www.biblestudy.org)

Paul's Jewish family was an Orthodox one. In fact, his father was a Pharisee (Acts 23:6). At an early age, probably after his bar mitzah at age 13, he was sent to school in Jerusalem where he studied the Torah under the guidance of Gamaliel, one of the most outstanding rabbis of his time (Acts 22:3). Gamaliel was a prestigious member of the Sanhedrin Council, the supreme Jewish council that established and regulated the religious laws of Israel (Acts 5:34).

Paul was very proud of his Jewish heritage. He described it in the following words: "[I was] circumcised the eighth day, of the nation of Israel, of the tribe of Benjamin, a Hebrew of Hebrews; as to the Law, a Pharisee . . . as to the righteousness which is in the Law, found blameless" (Philippians 3:5).

Paul's Response to the Church

It was no surprise, therefore, that when the Church was established in Jerusalem on the Day of Pentecost in about 30 AD, Paul responded with overwhelming passion to destroy it.

After all, it was made up of Jews who were claiming that the Messiah had come and had been murdered by the religious leaders of the Jewish nation (Acts 2:36). To Paul, this was absolute blasphemy, and he had no intention of allowing it to continue unchallenged.

And challenge it, he did. Years later, he referred to himself as one who was "furiously enraged" (Acts 26:11) and who persecuted the Church with "zeal" (Philippians 3:6). Acting under the authority of the Sanhedrin Council, He tracked down Christians, arrested them and supervised their execution. He described his activities in these words: "I persecuted this 'Way' [as Christians were called early in the Church's history] to the death, binding and delivering both men and women into prisons" (Acts 22:4).

He was so effective that the Sanhedrin authorized him to travel to the Syrian city of Damascus to find and arrest Christians who had fled from Jerusalem (Acts 9:1 and 22:3-5).

An Incredible Confrontation

On the way to Damascus, Paul experienced a dramatic, life-changing event. He was confronted by the resurrected Lord Jesus! Paul stated that this startling event took place at midday when he saw a great light from heaven, "brighter than the sun" that "flashed all around him (Acts 9:3 and 26:13). He then heard a voice that said, "Saul, Saul, why are you persecuting Me?" (Acts 9:4). Paul cried out, "Who are You, Lord?" The voice responded, "I am Jesus whom you are persecuting" (Acts 9:5). The men traveling with Paul saw the light and heard the voice, but unlike Paul, they saw no one (Acts 9:7).

Paul was told by Jesus, "I have appeared to you, to appoint you a servant and a witness . . . to the Gentiles . . . to open their eyes so that they may turn from darkness to light and from the authority of Satan to God, that they may receive forgiveness of sins and an inheritance among those who have been sanctified by faith in Me" (Acts 26:16-18). Paul, who had been blinded by the light, was then instructed to proceed to Damascus.

Paul's Conversion

Paul was led to Damascus by his accompanying men, and he spent the next "three days without sight, and neither ate nor drank" (Acts 9:9).

Meanwhile, the Lord had spoken to a Christian man in Damascus named Ananias, telling him to contact Paul at a certain house where he would find Paul praying (Acts 9:10-11).

Ananias was not the least thrilled by this message. In fact, he was terrified! Paul's reputation for murderous activities against Christians had preceded him (Acts 9:13-14). Accordingly, Ananias told the Lord he would prefer not to seek out Paul, but the Lord was insistent: "Go, for he is a chosen instrument of Mine, to bear My name before the Gentiles and kings and the sons of Israel" (Acts 9:15).

So, Ananias sought out Paul, laid hands on him and prayed for the restoration of his sight, which occurred immediately, He also prayed that Paul would be "filled with the Spirit" (Acts 9:17). Ananias then baptized Paul into the Christian community (Acts 9:18).

A Problem

Now, even though Ananias prayed that Paul would receive the Holy Spirit, which happened immediately, what happened after that indicates that Paul quenched the Spirit, which Christians are warned against specifically in 1 Thessalonians 5:19. A similar warning is found in Ephesians 4:30 where we are told not "to grieve the Spirit." Note that both of these warnings were written later in life by Paul, and he knew what he was talking about!

The Apostle Paul
by Rembrandt van Rijn (1606 -1669)

How do we quench or grieve the Holy Spirit? By refusing to allow Him on the throne of our life. This usually takes the form of relying on our talents and education instead of the power and guidance of the Spirit.

It appears this is exactly what Paul did, for we are told that he "immediately" began to proclaim Jesus in the synagogues of Damascus, attempting to prove that Jesus was the Messiah (Acts 9:20). No one can be saved one day and start preaching the next day without doing so in the flesh. New converts must pass through a process of sanctification whereby they come to know the Lord and His Word in a very personal and Spirit-led manner. That takes time.

Now, what I have to say next may shock you. Based upon Paul's behavior immediately following his conversion, I would suggest that he had a rather proud attitude that might be summarized in these words: "Lord, You are very fortunate to have me on Your side now. After all, I am a highly educated Orthodox Jew who knows the Torah backward and forward. As such, I will be able to nail the Jews to the wall with my theological training, combined with my talent for logical reasoning and debate."

You find that hard to believe? Well, let's consider what happened in response to Paul's preaching. No one was saved! Not a single person. Instead, he angered the Jews so much that they began to make plans to kill him (Acts 9:23).

Paul escaped their wrath by being lowered down over the city's walls at night in a large basket (Acts 9:25). Later in his life, while thinking back over the many indignities he had suffered during his ministry, Paul pointed to this escape as one of his most embarrassing moments — the night he became a "basket case"! (2 Corinthians 11:30-33).

A Continuing Problem

After his escape from Damascus, Paul decided to return to Jerusalem. Upon his arrival, he quickly made it clear that he had not learned anything from his bad experience in Damascus. Once again, he began to speak out "boldly" in the name of the Lord (Acts 9:28). He did so by "arguing" with the Jews (Acts 9:29).

The response was the same as it had been with the Jews in Damascus. They began to plot how they could "put him to death" (Acts 9:29).

At that point, the Christian brethren in Jerusalem decided that they were fed up with the trouble Paul was causing. They bought him a one-way ticket home and sent him away on a ship to his hometown of Tarsus.

What is said next is almost humorous. It is a sigh of relief on the part of the Israel churches (Acts 9:31):

> So the church throughout all Judea and Galilee and Samaria was having peace, being built

> up. And going on in the fear of the Lord and in the encouragement of the Holy Spirit, it continued to multiply.

Translation: "Praise God! We have finally gotten rid of that hot-headed troublemaker, Paul. Now, we can proceed to build up our churches in the love of Jesus."

The problem with Paul is that although he meant well, he was operating in the flesh and not in the power of the Holy Spirit. He had the internal dwelling of the Holy Spirit, but he was quenching the power of the Spirit in his life, relying instead on his own considerable talents and knowledge.

A Quiet Time

We do not hear of Paul again for 18 years! Three of those years Paul spent in Arabia on an unknown mission (Galatians 1:17). It may have been during this time that Paul was raptured to Heaven where he "heard inexpressible words, which a man is not permitted to speak" (2 Corinthians 12:1-4). It also could have been during this time that Paul received teaching directly from Jesus concerning the Gospel, as he explains in Galatians 1:

> 11) . . . the gospel which I am proclaiming as good news is not according to man.
>
> 12) For I neither received it from man, nor was I taught it, but I received it through a revelation of Jesus Christ.

Paul mentions his personal instruction from Jesus again in 1 Corinthians 11:23 where he says that his knowledge about the Last Supper and the institution of Communion was "received from the Lord."

In Galatians 2:1 Paul says that after the Jerusalem Christians sent him back to his hometown, he spent 14 years in Tarsus preaching and teaching. In Acts 11:25 we are told that

Barnabas came to Tarsus looking for Paul, and when he found him, he took him to Antioch where the disciples of Jesus were first called Christians. The two of them spent a year there teaching and preaching.

In summary, Paul spent 14 years in Tarsus, three in Arabia and one in Antioch. — a total of 18 years preparing for the ministry Jesus was going to entrust to him.

The Missionary Call

One day while the disciples at Antioch were ministering and fasting, the Holy Spirit spoke to them saying, "Set apart for Me Barnabas and Saul for the work to which I have called them" (Acts 13:1-2). The brethren fasted, laid their hands on them and prayed.

The book of Acts then tells us that Saul and Barnabas were "sent out by the Holy Spirit" . . . "to proclaim the word of God" (Acts 13:4-5) And it is specifically mentioned that "Saul, who was also known as Paul," was "filled with the Holy Spirit" (Acts 13:9). And thus, Paul was empowered to become the greatest missionary in the history of Christianity.

Why So Long?

Why did it take 18 years before Paul was anointed for the work that Jesus had called him to do? There were several reasons:

1) Paul had to get personally acquainted with Jesus through prayer, worship and studying the Hebrew Scriptures anew with a Christian worldview.

2) Paul's mind had to be delivered from the suffocating legalism of Judaism to the liberating grace of the Gospel.

3) Paul had to learn how to teach and preach the Scriptures in the power of the Spirit rather than by relying on his own power through fleshly debate.

It was only after Paul had surrendered the throne of his life to the Holy Spirit and submitted himself to sanctification that he was ready for the mission work the Lord had in mind for him.

From the Church's greatest enemy to its most successful promoter — that's what I call the life-changing power of Jesus!

The Apostle Paul

"I have been crucified with Christ, and it is no longer I who live, but Christ lives in me. And the life which I now live in the flesh I live by faith in the Son of God, who loved me and gave Himself up for me."

(Galatians 2:20)

Chapter 2

A Son of Thunder

"You will know the truth,
and the truth will make you free."
(John 8:32).

I was introduced to the Apostle John at a very early age when I read his glorious Gospel. I don't remember how old I was at the time, but I do remember that John's Gospel profoundly impacted me.

I was very fascinated by the fact that it was so different from the other Gospels. They began with Jesus's birth (Matthew and Luke) or with His baptism (Mark). In stark contrast, John started with Jesus in eternity past. The others presented chronologies of Jesus' life. John focused on discourses that emphasized Jesus' deity and His theology.

It became immediately apparent to me that John had a very deep personal relationship with Jesus. He also had a profound understanding of Jesus' nature and purpose that transcended the other Gospels.

I loved how John began his Gospel by making the bold declaration that "In the beginning, was the Word, and the Word was with God, and the Word was God . . . And the Word became flesh, and dwelt among us, and we beheld His glory, glory as of the only begotten from the Father, full of grace and truth" (John 1:1,14).

I was intrigued beyond measure by the words John used to conclude his Gospel: "And there are also many other things which Jesus did, which if they were written one after the other, I suppose that even the world itself could not contain the books that would be written" (John 21:25). I am still captivated by that statement, and accordingly, I look forward to hearing some of these stories when I have the blessing of meeting John personally in Heaven.

John Before Jesus

At this point, you may be wondering why I am including John in this book about people who were miraculously changed by their encounter with Jesus. The answer is simple. The fact is that John was radically changed by Jesus — just as was the Apostle Paul.

When John and his brother, James, were called by Jesus to be disciples of His, they were typical fishermen of that day and time. They were rugged individuals who were rash, raw, harsh and impetuous. They also proved to be very ambitious.

Let's consider three events in their lives that revealed their true nature early in their relationship with Jesus.

The first is in Mark 9:38-41, where we are told that while Jesus was teaching in Capernaum, John came to Him with a complaint about a man he had seen casting demons out of people in Jesus' name. John was upset because he declared that the man was not a member of Jesus' group of disciples.

Jesus responded to John's concern by gently rebuking him. He told John never to hinder anyone who was ministering in His name, for such a person would be unable to speak evil of Him. Jesus added: "For he who is not against us is for us. For whoever gives you a cup of water to drink in My name because you are of Christ, truly I say to you, he will not lose his reward."

A second example of John's need for sanctification to smooth off his rough edges is related in Mark 10:35-44. We are told that John came to Jesus with his brother, James, and asked Him to give them the seats of honor on the right and left of His throne when He began to reign over all the earth in glory. The request was a clear sign that the two brothers were consumed with ambition, and their request outraged the other disciples.

Once again, Jesus restrained Himself in His response. He told them that they did not understand what they were asking for. He explained that they were thinking like Gentiles who desired to exercise authority over others. He pointed out that His disciples would have to be very different from the world's rulers — that His followers must seek to serve rather than to rule (Mark 10):

> 43) ". . . whoever wishes to become great among you shall be your servant;
>
> 44) and whoever wishes to be first among you shall be slave of all.
>
> 45) For even the Son of Man did not come to be served, but to serve, and to give His life a ransom for many."

A third example of John's need for progressive sanctification is mentioned in Luke 9:51-54, where we are told that John and his brother became irate when a village of the Samaritans did not receive Jesus with open arms. They asked Jesus, "Lord, do You want us to command fire to come down from heaven and consume them?"

This time, the Lord's rebuke was more stern in nature. He quickly rejected their offer and stated that He had not "come to destroy men's lives, but to save them."

This incident makes it clear why Jesus gave the brothers the nickname of "Sons of Thunder" (Mark 3:17).

John After Jesus

We know that John's life was completely transformed by Jesus because by the time of his death, he was known as "The

The Apostle John by Russian-Ukrainian painter, Vladimir Borovikovsky (1757–1825).

Apostle of Love." It was a title well earned due to his first epistle in which he repeatedly encouraged the followers of Jesus to practice love:

> "Beloved, let us love one another, for love is from God; and everyone who loves has been born of God and knows God" (1 John 4:7).
>
> ". . . God is love, and the one who abides in love abides in God, and God abides in him" (1 John 4:16).
>
> "And this commandment we have from Him, that the one who loves God should love his brother also" (1 John 4:21).

Before writing his first epistle, John had already emphasized the importance of love by quoting a statement of Jesus which He delivered at The Last Supper: "This is My commandment, that you love one another, just as I have loved you" (John 13:34).

John also became known as a man of humility. He is the only Gospel writer to mention how Jesus washed the feet of His disciples at The Last Supper (John 13:5-16). Through this highly symbolic act, Jesus called His disciples to humility and servanthood. John got the message and passed it on,

Another characteristic of John is that he became passionately devoted to truth. He talked about the subject of truth more than any other Gospel writer. As Jesus was standing before Pilate, John records Jesus as saying, "I have come into the world, to bear witness to the truth" (John 18:37). John says that Pilate responded sarcastically to this statement by asking, "What is truth?" (John 18:38).

John's major concern in his Gospel was to convince the reader that Jesus truly was God in the flesh. He thus quoted Jesus as saying of Himself that He was God's "only begotten Son" (John 3:16). He presented seven great miracles Jesus performed to confirm His deity. He also provided seven "I Am" statements which the Jewish religious leaders recognized as claims of deity:

1) "I am the Bread of Life" (John 6:35).
2) "I am the Light of the World" (John 8:12).
3) "I am the Door" (John 10:9).
4) "I am the Good Shepherd" (John 10:11).
5) "I am the Resurrection and Life" (John 11:25).
6) "I am the Way, the Truth and the Life" (John 14:6).
7) "I am the True Vine" (John 15:1).

What a transformation John experienced!

One commentator has put it this way: "Jesus' love transformed John from a fire-calling zealot to a love-promoting father-figure."[1] Another summed up the change as "inward pride turned into outward humility."[2]

John's Final Service for the Lord

When John was in his 90s, he was arrested by the Roman Empire and sent to a prison colony on the Isle of Patmos, located about 35 miles off the west coast of modern-day Turkey.

Years ago when I sailed from Turkey to Patmos, I thought about how John must have felt when he made that same trip. I assumed that he must have been convinced that his life of service to the Lord had come to an end. After all, what could an extremely old man do for the Lord on a remote prison island, except perhaps witness to a few of the prisoners?

But John was about to experience one of the greatest events of his life, for soon after he arrived, Jesus appeared to him! It had been 60 years since the Lord's death and resurrection. Seeing Jesus again must have been the last thing John expected to experience. But he did — big time! He not only saw Jesus, but he saw Him with His heavenly glory restored, something he had gotten a glimpse of at the Transfiguration (Luke 9:28-36).

John was given the blessing of serving as the one to write the last book of the Bible — the book of Revelation. In this book, John was given an overview of end time events that contained great words of encouragement to the Lord's Church.

As the renowned British Evangelical, John Stott, summed it up:[3]

1) To a sinful church: "I know — Repent!"
2) To a doubtful church: "I have conquered — Believe!"
3) To a fearful church: "I am coming soon — Endure!"

I would add to this list one more message from the book of Revelation: To the end time church: "We win in the end — Rejoice!"

I thank Jesus for the great work of sanctification that He performed in the life of the Apostle John.

A Postscript

One final thought: when I was a student at the University of Texas many years ago in the mid-1950s, I noticed that engraved in stone above the entrance to the university's library were these words from the Apostle John's writings: "You shall know the truth, and the truth shall set you free" (John 8:32).

Those words, in that context, were highly misleading. They implied that students would find truth in the writings of men that were contained in that library.

Why were they misleading? Because the promise is based on a very important condition. That condition is expressed in the preceding verse which says, "If you abide in My word."

So, if you want to know truth — absolute truth — you must delve into God's Word, reading it, believing it and obeying it.

Psalm 1

> 1) How blessed is the man who does not walk
> in the counsel of the wicked,
> Nor stand in the way of sinners,
> Nor sit in the seat of scoffers!
>
> 2) But his delight is in the law of Yahweh,
> And in His law he meditates day and night.

The Apostle Paul

"For I am confident of this very thing, that He who began a good work in you will perfect it until the day of Christ Jesus."

(Philippians 1:6)

Chapter 3

A Tax Collector

> "No one can serve two masters; for either he will hate the one and love the other, or he will be devoted to one and despise the other. You cannot serve God and wealth."
> (Matthew 6:24)

In First Century Israel, tax collectors were considered the scum of the earth. Only prostitutes were held in greater disdain. Tax collectors were considered to be blood-sucking traitors to the nation. After all, they worked directly for the Romans who had the nation under occupation.

The video series called, "The Chosen," very accurately portrays how much the tax collectors were hated. When Jesus calls Matthew to be one of His disciples, His other disciples react in horror. After all, Matthew was not only a tax collector, but he was the official collector for the district that included the town of Capernaum, and therefore, he was the one who had enforced Roman taxes on several of the disciples who lived in that area and worked as fishermen.

Matthew is depicted in "The Chosen" as a very bright young man who lived in a mansion and who was hated so much that he feared assassination. Therefore, instead of walking to work each morning, he hires a man with an ox cart to take him to work while he is covered up in the cart so no one will see him!

Also, "The Chosen" reflects what surely must have been the ongoing attitude of Jesus' disciples. They are portrayed as highly resentful of Matthew, especially Peter. This leads to one of the most emotional scenes in the video series. Jesus convinces Peter that he must forgive Matthew, and the impulsive Peter responds by rushing to a gathering of the disciples where he suddenly embraces Matthew and audibly forgives him in front of the others.

Another highly emotional scene takes place when Matthew decides to go to his father and mother to ask them to forgive him. They have suffered greatly by being ostracized by their neighbors and friends for being Matthew's parents. His father, at first, wants nothing to do with him, but both of his parents finally come around and are reconciled to him.

These are not scenes recorded in the Bible, but they are highly believable, considering the attitude of intense hostility that existed toward tax collectors.

Jesus' Attitude

Jesus was constantly criticized for socializing and eating with tax collectors. Matthew himself records such an occasion in his Gospel, pointing out that Jesus was severely attacked for eating with tax collectors. He records Jesus' response as follows (Matthew 9):

> 12) But when Jesus heard this, He said, "It is not those who are healthy who need a physician, but those who are sick.
>
> 13) But go and learn what this means: 'I desire compassion, and not sacrifice,' for I did not come to call the righteous, but sinners."

In one of His well-known parables, Jesus compared a Pharisee with a tax collector (Luke 18:9-14). He said that two men went up to the Temple to pray — a Pharisee and a tax collector. The Pharisee thanked God that he was not a sinner like the tax collector, whereas the tax collector prayed, "God, be merciful to me a sinner!" Jesus concluded that the tax

The Apostle Matthew
Leonardo da Vinci (1452-1519)

collector returned to his home justified before God because "everyone who exalts himself shall be humbled, but he who humbles himself shall be exalted." (Luke 18:14).

To exalt a tax collector above a Pharisee was a shocking teaching. The Pharisee represented the elite of society. The tax collector was at the bottom of the social strata. It was this kind of teaching that infuriated the Pharisees and finally drove them to conspire to kill Jesus.

The Nature and Status of Tax Collectors

Tax collectors had to be educated in both mathematics and accounting, They also had to be fluent in several languages, like Hebrew, Aramaic, Greek and Latin.

Additionally, they had to have substantial personal financial resources because they got control of their tax territory by presenting the Romans with the highest bid. To make up for this up-front money, they skimmed money off the top for themselves by adding a percentage to the taxes collected. This was known to the general public, which caused them to be hated even more.[1]

Rabbis held tax collectors in utter contempt. The Babylonian Talmud equated tax collectors with "murderers and robbers." Rabbis taught that tax collectors should be treated as social outcasts and should be disqualified from serving as witnesses in court. Many rabbis excommunicated tax collectors from their synagogues. Rabbis even ruled it was lawful for people to lie in any conceivable way to avoid or lessen their payment of taxes.[2]

One expert concluded that being a tax collector for the Romans would be like Billy Graham hiring a staff member who was a member of a Mexican cartel![3]

Again, when you consider how tax collectors were held in such contempt, you can better understand why the Pharisees became so enraged when Jesus would compare the tax collectors favorably above them.

For example, Matthew tells in his Gospel that on an occasion when Jesus went to the Temple and was confronted by "the chief priests and the elders of the people," He said to them, "Truly, I say to you that the tax collectors and prostitutes will get into the kingdom of God before you" (Matthew 21:23 & 31). That statement must have warmed the heart of a former tax collector like Matthew!

The Call and Transformation of Matthew

And so, a tax collector named Matthew was called by Jesus to be on His team of disciples, and three years with Jesus totally changed his life. He was delivered from his greed which had made money his idol.

The Bible indicates that his original name was "Levi the son of Alphaeus" (Mark 2:14 and Luke 5:27). Matthew is likely the name that Jesus gave him. It meant, "Gift of Yahweh."[4]

I've always been fascinated by the fact that the Bible says Jesus was just walking by Matthew's tax office one day when

He suddenly called the tax collector to follow Him, and Matthew immediately dropped everything, including his lucrative job, and just walked away with Jesus.

Why such a sudden and radical response? The only thing I can think of is a statement in 2 Chronicles 16:9 which says: "For the eyes of Yahweh move to and fro throughout the earth that He may strongly support those whose heart is wholly devoted to Him . . ." This statement leads me to believe that Matthew had furtively heard some of Jesus' messages, and his heart had been deeply touched.

Nothing else is known about the life of Matthew, although early Church historians passed along a tradition that he was martyred while preaching in Ethiopia.[5]

Matthew's Gospel

His Gospel is the longest and the most comprehensive about the life of Jesus. It was aimed at the Jews for the purpose of convincing them that Jesus was the promised Messiah. Thus, it begins with a detailed genealogy that traces Jesus' heritage back to Abraham through David. It also contains more references from the Hebrew Scriptures than any other Gospel — the purpose being to prove that Jesus' birth, life, ministry, death and resurrection were all fulfillments of Jewish prophecies.

The Gospel is organized around five discourses that are related in detail:[6]

1) The Sermon on the Mount (Matthew 5-7).
   Containing the central tenets of Christian discipleship.

2) The Little Commission Discourse (Matthew 10).
   Directed at the 12 Apostles on how to conduct themselves in their mission work.

3) The Parabolic Discourse (Matthew 13).
   In which Jesus uses seven parables to teach about

God's Kingdom.

4) The Discourse on the Church (Matthew 18). Instructions about how to lead the Church.

5) The Olivet Discourse (Matthew 23-25). Prophecies concerning the End Times.

These discourses, particularly The Sermon on the Mount, are recorded in such detail that they leave the impression that Matthew must have written them in shorthand — a quick form of note taking that had been developed in Rome about 60 years before Jesus and which most tax collectors were proficient in using.[7]

Another Tax Collector

Zacchaeus in the Sycamore Tree
by The French painter, James Tissot (1836-1902).

There is a story in the Gospels about another tax collector who had an equally radical conversion to Jesus as did Matthew (Luke 19:1-10). His name was Zacchaeus, and he was the chief tax collector in Jericho. Like most tax collectors, the Bible says he was a rich man. He heard Jesus was coming to town, and since he was a short man, he ran ahead and climbed a tree to make certain he could see Jesus as He passed.

To Zacchaeus' absolute shock, Jesus stopped when He got to the tree, looked up and said, "Zacchaeus, hurry and come down, for today I must stay at your house." In modern day terms, it would have to be said that Zacchaeus was "freaked out!" He replied to Jesus, "Behold, half of my possessions, Lord, I will give to the poor, and if I have extorted anyone of anything, I will give back four times as much." Jesus responded by declaring, "Today salvation has come to this house, because he, too, is a son of Abraham. For the Son of Man has come to seek and to save the lost."

And so, when it comes to the outcasts of society, we have two examples of tax collectors being received by Jesus and then being radically changed in the process.

Praise God for Jesus' life-changing power that is still in operation today!

The Apostle Paul

"Now may the God of peace Himself sanctify you entirely, and may your spirit and soul and body be preserved complete, without blame at the coming of our Lord Jesus Christ."

(1 Thessalonians 5:23)

Historical Examples

Chapter 4

A Slave Trader

"Wretched man that I am!
Who will deliver me from the body of this death?"
(Romans 7:24)

When I began my study of John Newton's life, the only thing I knew about him was that he was a former slave ship captain who became a Christian and then wrote the hymn, *Amazing Grace*, which ultimately became one of the greatest classics of Christian music. I was, therefore, greatly shocked when I discovered the degree of moral depravity to which he sank in his early life.

His definitive biography by Jonathan Aitken contains a foreword written by Philip Yancey. It ends with the observation that the life of John Newton is an illustration of the truth that "Grace, like water, always flows downward, to the lowest level."[1]

Seriously, you had better put on your seat belt because you are about to read a jaw-dropping story.

A Stellar Beginning

Actually, John's life got off to a good start. He was born on August 4, 1725, in a suburb of London, England. He was named after his father who made his living as the captain of a merchant ship. His father's voyages took nine months to a year, so John hardly knew his father when he was a child.

The result was that John was raised by his mother, Elizabeth. She was a loving and caring mom who doted on her son. John was a very precocious child who was reading by the age of three. He also had an amazing memory, and by the age of five, he had memorized the Westminster Shorter Catechism. His mother also had him reading classics of the Christian faith. She told her son repeatedly that her goal for his life was for him to attend a seminary and become a clergyman.

His mother took him to a Dissenter church where he heard passionate peaching and was introduced to the hymns of Isaac Watts who lived nearby and would sometimes come to the church to introduce new songs. John's favorite hymn was "When I Survey the Wondrous Cross."

John's father was more traditional when it came to religion, and so when he was home, he always took John to an Anglican church. John was thus introduced to a variety of Christian traditions.

With his sharp mind, his mother's love and tutoring and his father's fine job, John's future looked good indeed. But all that was to change very suddenly.

Disaster

Shortly before John was due to turn seven years old, his mother suddenly died of cancer. She had been his constant companion, teacher and playmate. Her loss was devastating.

His father was at sea when his mother died. John did not know what to expect from his father since he hardly knew him. He was a stern and humorless man, and John feared him.

John suffered another shock a few weeks after his father returned home when His father informed him that he was remarrying to a farmer's daughter, and that he intended to move to the countryside.

The move cast John into a whole new environment. His new stepmother could not read or write and had no interest in teaching John anything except how to do farm chores. She was not a praying woman, and she seldom went to church.

John's father decided to deal with John in his long seafaring absences by putting him in a boarding school. John hated the school and spent only two years there before his father changed his mind and decided that John had gotten enough education.

Introduction to Sailing

His father decided that John would be better off sailing with him, serving as a cabin boy. John was 10 years old in 1735 when he departed with his father on a voyage to Spain and then on to Italy. The round trip would take nine months.

This was to prove to be a terrible decision on the part of his father. I know this from first hand experience because when I was 12 years old, I went to work in the summer for my dad in one of his businesses — a sheet metal shop. The men I worked with were rough and tough. Their language was despicable, and they spent every lunch time bragging about their sexual conquests.

This kind of exposure to the evils of the world had a very negative impact on me. But my exposure was for eight hours a day, five days a week. Ten year old John was thrown in with salty sailors 24 hours a day, every day, for almost a year. John soon learned that being a young practicing Christian on board a merchant ship was very unpopular and led to mockery.

On his next voyage, John's father decided not to take John along for some unknown reason. Perhaps he realized the negative effect that being with sailors was having on his son.

While his father was gone, John fell in with a bad crowd and got into constant trouble. This convinced his father to take him on his next voyage to Southern Europe.

When he returned home in 1738 at age 13, he had a near-death experience. He had an appointment with two friends to row out to a warship that was anchored in a nearby port. He arrived late and found that his friends had already departed.

While watching them row to the ship, they hit a floating log and tipped over. Both of his friends drowned. Newton realized that if he had been with them, he would have also drowned because he did not know how to swim. This tragedy drove him back to reading his Bible and praying.

Soon after the funeral of his friends, John's father announced that he wanted his son to accompany him on another voyage around the Mediterranean. This time he went as a crew member and thus lived below deck with the sailors who were constantly carousing. John's desire at age 15 to live a godly life quickly dissipated. His life below decks coarsened him and he began drinking heavily and cursing constantly. In fact, he came to be considered the worst blasphemer on board.

Two years later, afer the completion of another voyage, John's father announced that he had arranged for his son to become a slave overseer on a Jamaican plantation.

John liked the idea, but before departing, his father asked him to travel 30 miles by horseback to deliver some legal papers. In the process, he decided to visit the home of one of his mother's cousins.

An Important Visit

That stopover was to have a major impact on John's life. He was 17 at the time when he met the 13 year old daughter of his mother's cousin. Her name was Polly, and John was captivated by her. Three weeks later, John was still there! The result was that he missed his ship to Jamaica.

His father was enraged, and he responded to John's irresponsibility by signing him up as a crew member on a ship headed to Italy. This was John's first voyage on a ship that was not captained by his father, and he soon discovered he was treated differently The sailors were more brutal and depraved when they were around him.

Disaster Again

John survived the eleven-month voyage, arriving back in London in December of 1743 when he was 18 years old. He had a joyous opportunity to see Polly once again, but in March of 1744, he was suddenly shanghaied! It occurred one day as he was strolling along the waterfront of a port.

He was captured by what was called a Royal Navy "press-gang." Under British law at that time, such kidnappings were legal during war or when there was a threat of war — and war was looming between Britain and France.

The warship John was assigned to contained many criminals among its crew. They had been sentenced to naval service instead of prison. Once again, John found himself in a very depraved atmosphere.

When John learned one day that his ship had been ordered to escort a convoy of merchant ships headed to India, he decided to take decisive action. Such a voyage would take five years, and he could not fathom being gone from Polly that long. So, in March 1745, he deserted his ship before it could begin its long journey.

He was quickly recaptured and found himself facing a death sentence. Probably due to the fact that his father was a well known sea captain, the captain of his warship decided not to seek the death penalty. Instead, he ordered John to receive 24 lashes with a cat-ó-nine-tails.

In April of 1745, John's warship set sail for Madeira, a Portuguese island in the Atlantic Ocean, located about 400 miles west of the coast of Morocco in North Africa. The ship was still under command to escort a convoy to Italy, and John was heartsick over having to face such a long absence from Polly.

When John's ship reached the island of Madeira, he noticed that there was a number of merchant ships anchored there, and he got an idea. He approached his captain and asked that he trade him for one of the merchant marine sailors. This was a common practice at that time. His captain jumped at the idea because he wanted to get rid of John who had proven to be a constant trouble maker.

When the trade was consummated, John found himself on a slave ship that was headed to the west coast of Africa to pick up slaves to be taken to Jamaica and Barbados. Onboard, John met an Englishman named Amos who was a professional slave trader. He filled John's head with stories about the fortunes that could be made in the slave trading business, and John was enthralled.

On New Year's Day in 1746, while the ship was anchored off the west coast of Africa, the captain of the ship suddenly died. The new captain was a man that John had vilified and made into an enemy. John immediately realized he was in great trouble. He knew the new captain would take delight in trading him back to a British navy ship.

A Bad Decision

John made a quick decision to abandon the ship and cast his lot with his new friend, Amos. He dreamed of making lots of money quickly in the slave trade and returning to England to marry Polly.

At first, things went well with Amos. But then, one day Amos returned from a slave-trading trip with an African woman whom he introduced as his wife. She took an instant dislike of John.

Shortly thereafter, Amos and John started making plans to travel along the coast to buy slaves, but before they could depart, John became very ill with what was called "white man's fever." This was a malady that often caused death.

Amos decided to proceed with the planned trip, so he left John behind. Immediately after his departure, Amos' wife took action and enslaved John in chains. She started slowly starving him to death. His condition became so grave that the African slaves took pity on him and started sneaking him bits of food each evening.

When Amos returned, his wife fed him a bunch of lies about how she had discovered that John was plotting to take over his business, and he believed her. So Amos decided to keep John in chains, and he began to work him as one of his slaves.

John decided that his only hope for survival was to get a letter to his father. Over the next few months, he wrote three letters to his dad, asking him to alert his fellow sea captains to search for him and bring him home. These letters were sneaked into Amos' outgoing mailbag by John's fellow slaves.

In December of 1746, John was suddenly delivered from his slavery when Amos traded him to another slave master who had a base about 100 miles down the coast. His new master wanted John to be the manager of his operation. It proved to be an ideal job, and John was soon making significant money.

This was the period when John hit rock bottom spiritually and morally. John quickly became mentally hardened to the gruesome practice of slavery. He also "grew black" — a term used to describe Europeans who settled among the African natives and assimilated into their culture.

Accordingly, John began to force himself sexually on his female slaves, and he began to dabble in witchcraft! In short, John was wallowing in debauchery and enjoying every moment of it.

A Surprise

A year later, 21 year old John was suddenly confronted with an English sea captain of a merchant ship. It turned out that John's dad had actually received one of his letters. He had responded by alerting all his sea captain friends to be on the lookout for John when they were anywhere near Africa.

The captain announced that he had come to rescue John and take him back home to England. To his astonishment, John showed no interest in going home! After all, John felt like he was sitting on top of the world with his lucrative slave trading operation.

That's when the captain told John that he had received a very large fortune due to an inheritance he had received from a distant relative of his mother. That was music to John's ears, and he decided to go home.

A Life-Changing Voyage

The ship John boarded, called the *Greyhound*, was not a slave ship. It was plying the coast of Africa for items like ivory, gold and sandalwood. Since John was a guest passenger and had no seaman duties, he had plenty of spare time. He spent that time reading every secular book on the ship.

When he finished all these, the only book left was a religious classic titled, *The Imitation of Christ*. It was written in the 1400s by Thomas à Kempis, a German priest. The book's devotional messages disturbed and distressed John because he had "long since decided the Bible and the God it spoke of was a myth."[2]

John had manifested his ungodly attitude throughout the voyage by drinking heavily, using blasphemous language and engaging in hell-raising. In the process he had alienated the captain.

The morning after he had read the Christian classic, he

was awakened by someone shouting,"The ship is sinking!" And sure enough, it was. The ship had encountered a severe storm during the night, and a high wave had knocked a hole in the hull. The ship was taking on water fast.

John quickly jumped out of bed and discovered that the entire crew was engaged in pumping and bailing water. This frantic activity continued for hours while John helped at the helm. At one point, John yelled out, "Lord, have mercy on us!"[3] Those words shocked both him and the captain.

Finally, the storm abated. It was then discovered that all the food on the ship had either been swept overboard or else ruined by the seawater. The entire crew faced starvation.

But a favorable wind suddenly sprung up, and the ship started drifting toward Ireland. On April 8, 1748, the *Greyhound* limped into an Irish port. John later wrote that when he stepped ashore, "about this time I began to know that there is a God who hears and answers prayers."[4] His most definitive modern day biographer states, "It was the time of John Newton's conversion."[5]

John had returned to the Savior he had abandoned as a youth. He now stood justified before God, forgiven of his sins. But he had a long road of sanctification yet to go.

Milestones of Sanctification

John's faith in Jesus immediately convicted him of the need to cease his gambling, swearing and drunkenness. But it would be several years before he became repentant of making his living as a slave trader.

In fact, after his conversion, he continued in the slave trading business for six years, making a total of four voyages to Africa — the first one while serving as first mate and the remaining ones as captain. He was granted the rank of captain in 1750 at the age of 25!

John was deterred from making any further voyages by a sudden, mysterious brain seizure he experienced in 1755. At that same time, his wife, Polly, whom he had finally married in 1750, became seriously ill. John took these events as a sign from God that he should surrender his seafaring career.

Through a bizarre series of circumstances that could only be classified as miraculous, John received an appointment to serve as the "tide surveyor" in the port of Liverpool. John was astounded by this development. He suddenly found himself with a staff of 60 and an excellent salary. His role was to see to the taxation of the cargos of all incoming ships. He knew his income would be doubled by "stokes," which were bribes to overlook smuggled goods.

Meanwhile, John was rigorously studying the Bible, keeping an extensive prayer journal, reading theology books, learning Latin and Greek and visiting a variety of churches to hear sermons by many kinds of preachers — both Anglican and Dissidents (Methodists, Presbyterians, Baptists and Moravians).

Two Dissidents in particular grabbed John's attention and affection, and he became personal friends with both — John Wesley and George Whitefield. Through their preaching, the Holy Spirit began to work mightily on John's conscience.

First, he decided to abandon the taking of stokes, and ordered that his staff do likewise. This cut his income in half and infuriated all his staff members. Second, he began to feel remorse for his involvement in the slave trade.

God's Call

Gradually, John felt called of God to full-time ministry, but he was torn between whether he should be ordained by the Dissidents or the Anglicans. He preferred the Dissidents because of their passionate preaching, but his wife and her influential parents insisted that he seek ordination by the

John Newton

Anglican Church.

So, John finally decided to go with the Anglicans. He made application and was rejected. His rejection was based on the fact that he did not have a university degree, although many exceptions had been made to this rule. The real reason was his close association with Dissidents.

John did not give up easily. He persisted for six years, and was finally ordained by the Anglican Church in March of 1764 when he was 38 years old.

He was to spend the next 43 years of his life in full-time ministry, first at a small village church for 16 years and then a large church located in the financial district of London for 27 years.

During those years, John became a celebrity. People loved his passionate preaching and his gifted hymn writing. But what really made him famous was his autobiography (1764) and his hymnal (1799), both of which became best sellers.

Political Impact

It was in December of 1785 that John made contact with a young member of Parliament named William Wilberforce. John was 60 years old and William was 26. But despite their age difference, the two developed a strong friendship over the following years as they joined forces to get legislation passed that would outlaw slave trading. It would prove to be a long and arduous fight — not culminating in success for 22 years in February of 1807.

John played a key role in this fight. In 1788, he published a booklet titled, *Thoughts Upon the African Salve Trade*. It provided a graphic description of the horrors of the slave trade. It spread like wild fire and had the same impact on British public opinion about slavery as did *Uncle Tom's Cabin* some 60 years later when it was published in the United States (1852).

Conclusion

John's dear wife, whom he loved with all his heart, died of cancer in 1790 at the age of 59 after 40 years of marriage. John was called home to the Lord on December 21, 1802, at the age of 82 — in a time when the life expectancy of a man was 45 years. Shortly before his death, John made this observation about his life: "My memory is nearly gone, but I remember two things: I am a great sinner and Christ is a great Savior."[6]

John wrote his own epitaph:[7]

John Newton
once an infidel and libertine,
a servant of slaves in Africa,
was by the rich mercy of
our Lord and Savior Jesus Christ
preserved, restored, pardoned
and appointed to preach the faith
he had long labored to destroy.

Chapter 5

An Oxford Professor

"Sanctify Christ as Lord in your hearts,
always being ready to make a defense
to everyone who asks you to give an account
for the hope that is in you,
yet with gentleness and fear."
(1 Peter 3:15)

Clive Staples Lewis was one of the greatest defenders of the Christian faith during the 20th Century, despite the fact that he did not become a Christian until he was 32 years old — and before that time, he was an Atheist.[1]

His unusual name was evidently one he did not like because at age four, he suddenly announced that from that point on, he wanted to be called Jackie. As he grew older, Jackie evolved into Jack, and the rest of his life, all his family, friends and acquaintances called him Jack. To most Americans today, however, he is simply known as C. S. Lewis.

Jack was born in Belfast, Northern Ireland in November 1898. He was his parent's second son. The first was three years older, having been born in 1895. His name was Warren, but his nickname by which he was known throughout his life was Warnie. The boys' mother, Flora, was the daughter of a Church of Ireland pastor. Their father, Albert, was a lawyer. They were an upper middle class family.

The brothers grew up as very close buddies, and they remained dear friends throughout their lifetimes. They were educated at home by their mother who taught them French and Latin. A governess taught them other subjects. Their father was aloof and had the temperament of a worrier.

A Great Family Disaster

In 1908, Jack's mother had surgery for cancer. She lingered for several months before she died. Jack prayed earnestly for her healing. But his prayers were of no avail. Her death devastated him. He even prayed for a miracle to bring her back alive. Jack was only 10 years old.

Jack's father was also shattered by his wife's death. He began to manifest temper tantrums as he seemed to be at his wit's end as to what to do with his sons. In 1908, he finally decided to send them to a private school located near London.

A Struggling Educational Experience

The school turned out to be a nightmare experience for both boys. In past years it had been known for its excellence. Jack's father was unaware that its reputation had become nefarious due to the cruel conduct of its headmaster.

Jack complained to his father that the school had "disgusting food," "stinking sanitation," "cold beds" and "almost no teaching."[2] The boys were beaten unmercifully. But their father ignored their complaints, and Jack was scarred for life. The school was closed in 1910, and the headmaster was confined to an insane asylum!

Most of Jack's education in his early years was self-taught through extensive reading. Jack's parents were readers, and their house was filled with books. Jack devoured them, and he continued to read exhaustively after leaving home.

Jack had a very strong sense of rectitude, and he began to suffer guilt over his sins. He developed a morbid fear of Hell. He prayed, but he found no solace.

As he studied history, he began to learn about the religions of ancient Greece and Rome. He became skeptical about Christianity and convinced that the Bible was full of myths and superstitions. He finally decided there was no Hell, nor was there a God. So, at age 15, he announced to friends that he had become an Atheist.

After two years at his initial boarding school, Jack was transferred to a high school called Malvern College that was located near London. His brother was already there. This school proved to be a waste of time for Jack because its focus was sports, which Warnie excelled in, but Jack abhorred. Jack was so miserable at the school that he insisted that his father allow him to leave.

In September of 1914, Jack's father decided to transfer his son to a highly respected private tutor located in a village near London. Jack lived with the tutor and his wife at their home. This tutor proved to be the first real teacher in Jack's life.

He challenged Jack to think logically, he taught him languages and urged the boy (he was 15 at the time) to read profusely. Jack began to develop an intense interest in Norse mythology.

Unfortunately, Jack's tutor was an Atheist, so he contributed nothing to the boy's positive spiritual development. Instead, he endorsed Jack's Atheism. It was during this time that Jack wrote a friend that he was "quite content to live without believing in a bogy who is prepared to torture me forever and ever if I should fail in coming up to an almost impossible ideal."[3]

In 1914, Jack's father arranged for him to be confirmed at the family church in Belfast. Jack could not bring himself to confess to his father that he was no longer a believer, so he went through with the ceremony. Later, he regarded his confirmation to be "one of the worst acts of my life, combining cowardice with blasphemy."[4] To his best friend he wrote: "All religions, that is, all mythologies to give the proper name, are merely man's own inventions."[5]

But there was already a strange tension in Jack's intellectual life. He professed to be an Atheist, but increasingly, he found that his favorite books were written by Christians like George MacDonald and John Bunyan.

What Career?

Meanwhile Jack's father was becoming increasingly concerned about his son's future. What career should he pursue?

His father wanted him to become a lawyer. His brother, Warnie, had chosen the military and entered a military academy. Jack's tutor told his father that the only thing his son was fitted for was to become a scholar. Jack wanted to be a poet.

His father and his tutor finally agreed that Jack should seek a scholarship to Oxford, which he did, and which he received in 1916 when he was 17.

A Complicating Factor

Meanwhile, the First World War, which had broken out in July 1914, was raging across Europe and overshadowing everything. There were only ten men in Jack's Oxford class when he entered in the Spring of 1917 because so many young men were serving in the war.

Warnie was already in Europe on the front lines. Jack faced that prospect soon because British law required all men to enlist in the military at age 18. Jack could have asked for an exemption since he was from Northern Ireland, and his father encouraged him to do so, but he refused. Jack felt it would be dishonorable for him to refuse to serve.

So, Jack entered the officer's training program in June of 1917, only a couple of months after entering Oxford. In November, he was suddenly sent to the front lines.

Jack quickly developed a case of "trench fever," and he had to be hospitalized. Jack spent his time reading every book he could get his hands on. It was during this time that he was introduced to the writings of G. K. Chesterton. He felt a kinship with the man although Jack had no idea he was a Christian. In later years, Jack looked back on his reading of George MacDonald and Chesterton and quipped, "A young man who wishes to remain an Atheist cannot be too careful of his reading."[6]

In April 1918, Jack was wounded by an artillery shell. It was discovered that one of the pieces of shrapnel had lodged in his chest, and the wound was declared serious enough to excuse him from combat.

Returning Home

In June of 1919, Jack returned to Oxford to resume his studies. By this time, his family situation had changed radically.

While he had been in officer training school, Jack and his roommate, Paddy Moore, had exchanged promises that if either was killed in the war, the surviving one would take over the responsibility for the other's parents.

Subsequently, Jack's roommate was killed, and Jack kept his promise by assuming responsibility for his roommate's mother. In the years that followed, Mrs. Moore filled the void left by the death of Jack's own mother, and he began to rely on her care and comfort.

In the process, Jack's relationship with his father became even more remote. Part of the reason was the fact that his father had become an alcoholic and was severely depressed. His father died of cancer in 1929.

Meanwhile, Jack excelled at his studies, focusing on Medieval English. He was obviously a genius and he was offered a teaching fellowship at Oxford's Magdalen College in May of 1925, at age 26.

The Turning Point

When Jack took up residence at Magdalen (as instructors were required to do), he began to meet intellectuals who were Believers, the most influential being J. R. R. Tolkien, the man who would write *The Lord of the Rings* (1954-1955). As he interacted with these men, Jack began to wrestle with God. One day, in the summer of 1929, Jack got on a double-decker bus, and while he was riding, he decided to "open the door" to God. He was 30 years old.

Here's how Jack described that moment: "I gave in and admitted that God was God."[7] Later that night, he got on his knees and prayed. As he did so, he said he was "the most dejected and reluctant convert in all England."[8]

Jack did not yet believe in Jesus, but he had taken the first step in that direction by accepting the existence of God. The amazing thing is that his journey was being propelled by logic and Christian writers, rather than preachers and the Scriptures. At this point, Jack felt "that Christianity was very sensible, apart from Christianity."[9] He meant that he feared the consequences of putting his faith in Jesus because he knew it would result in changes in his life.

Finally, two years later, Jack took the plunge. It happened on September 28, 1931, when he went to the zoo with his brother, riding in a side car attached to his brother's motorcycle. Jack later wrote, "I did not believe that Jesus Christ was the Son of God, and when I reached the zoo, I did."[10] He was 32 years old. In December of 1931, he took communion for the first time.

The New Man in Christ

Jack immediately threw himself into Christian writing. In a two week period of time in 1932, he wrote *The Pilgrim's Regress* which was published in 1933. Very soon, a group of Christian writers, including Tolkien, started meeting weekly

C. S. Lewis
(https://en.wikipedia.org)

at a pub to discuss their writings. Jack named the group, The Inklings.

Simultaneously, Jack's academic career flourished in 1936 when he published *The Allegory of Love* — a study of love poetry in the Middle Ages. He also became a very popular lecturer at Oxford.

Meanwhile, Jack continued feverishly writing books designed for the general public. In doing so, he evidenced a wide range of interests and topics. For example, his next book was a science fiction novel with a Christian perspective. It was the first of three he would write over the years.

But Jack's focus soon became a defense of his new-born faith. His first attempt at apologetics was a book titled, *The Problem of Pain*, which was published in 1940, when he was

40 years old. In subsequent years, he wrote a book on miracles, one on death and another on Heaven.

But his first blockbuster was *The Screwtape Letters* (1942). It was a witty, insightful book about human nature as presented in letters from a senior demon to a junior one. This book was so profound that it resulted in Jack's picture on the cover of *Time* magazine.

Jack's most influential worldwide classic resulted from an invitation from the BBC (British Broadcasting Corporation) to give a series of radio talks on Christianity to encourage the British people in the midst of World War II. The talks proved to be enormously popular, and after the war, they were consolidated into the book titled, *Mere Christianity* (1952).

Jack's fame and success backfired on him because his fellow professors became jealous of him. They looked for every opportunity to criticize him. In the process, they refused to allow him to gain a full professorship. One of their criticisms was that a true scholar would never stoop to writing for the general public. Jack finally got fed up with this nonsense, and in 1954 he transferred to Cambridge University where he was given the prestigious Chair of Medieval and Renaissance English.

The Final Years

Jack's spiritual autobiography was titled, *Surprised by Joy* (1955). It focuses on his path to faith in Jesus. The title proved prophetic because near the end of his life, in 1956, he married an American poet named Joy Davidman. Two months after their marriage, she was diagnosed with terminal cancer. She died four years later in 1960 at the age of 45.

Jack died three years after Joy on November 22, 1973 — the day that President John F. Kennedy was assassinated. Jack's death was overshadowed by the President's, and it was some time before many people discovered that Jack had died suddenly of a heart attack.

A Lasting Legacy

To this day, Jack remains one of the most quoted Christian authors of the 20th Century. This is due mainly to the rigorous logic he always demonstrated in his books. Perhaps his most famous words are those he wrote in *Mere Christianity* about the divinity of Jesus:[11]

> I am trying here to prevent anyone saying the really foolish thing that people often say about Him: "I'm ready to accept Jesus as a great moral teacher, but I don't accept His claim to be God." That is the one thing we must not say. A man who was merely a man and said the sort of things that Jesus said would not be a great moral teacher. He would either be a lunatic — on a level with the man who says that he is a poached egg — or else he would be the Devil of Hell. You must make your choice. Either this man was, and is, the Son of God, or else a madman or something worse. You can shut Him up for a fool, you can spit at Him and kill Him as a demon, or you can fall at His feet and call Him Lord and God. But let us not come with any patronizing nonsense about His being a great human teacher. He has not left that open to us. He did not intend to.

C. S. Lewis

“Give up your self, and you will find your real self. Lose your life and you will save it. Submit to death, death of your ambitions and favorite wishes every day and death of your whole body in the end: submit with every fibre of your being, and you will find eternal life. Keep back nothing. Nothing that you have not given away will ever be really yours. Nothing in you that has not died will ever be raised from the dead. Look for yourself, and you will find in the long run only hatred, loneliness, despair, rage, ruin and decay. But look for Christ and you will find Him, and with Him everything else thrown in.

(*Mere Christianity*)

Chapter 6

A Jewish Communist

"Don't copy the behavior and customs of this world, but let God transform you into a new person by changing the way you think. Then you will learn to know God's will for you, which is good and pleasing and perfect."
(Romans 12:2 — NLT)

Some stories are so amazing that they are truly stranger than fiction. This story is one of those. It is true, but it would be beyond the imagination of a novelist or screen writer. It is the story of the life of Helen Joy Davidman.

Joy, as she was always called, was born in the Bronx in 1915 to second generation Jewish immigrants from Poland and Russia. Her parents were both educators in the New York City public school system. Her father was a principal, and her mother was an elementary school teacher.

A Bright But Rebellious Girl

Joy's parents naturally took a special interest in her education from the moment she was born, and they very quickly discovered that she was a child prodigy with a photographic memory. She was a voracious reader and had read H. G. Wells' Outline of History by the time she was 9 years old. At age 12 she announced to her parents that she was an Atheist. That didn't upset them because they had both become secular Jews who were more interested in being Americanized than in maintaining the religion of their forefathers.

Joy started writing poetry and short stories at an early age and was becoming an accomplished writer by the time she entered Hunter College at the age of 15. Within a year she had her first sexual liaison with a professor who was old enough to be her father. Shortly after that encounter, she announced that she no longer believed in standards of right and wrong. She referred to moral codes as "ugly things" and declared, "I've converted to Hedonism."[1]

At age 19, Joy was accepted as a graduate student at Columbia University where she began working on a Master's degree in English Literature, with a minor in French. She completed that degree in a year's time.

Spectacular Literary Success

Upon graduation, Joy began teaching high school — a job she hated. She poured herself into writing and had several of her poems accepted for publication in the prestigious *Poetry* magazine.

In 1938, Joy received word from Yale University that she had won the Yale Younger Poet's Award. This award brought her national attention and confirmed her intention to become a professional writer.

But an even greater accolade was to come. In January of 1939, at age 24, she was given the poetry prize by the National Institute of Arts and Letters. The first recipient of this prize had been Robert Frost in 1931.

A Difficult Person

Joy had always been a socially awkward person. Combine that with her rebellious spirit and condescending intellect and you end up with a personality that was intolerable to most people. The awards made the situation even worse as her ego got out of hand.

Words people used to describe her included aggressive, impertinent, intolerant, opinionated, rebellious, pompous, impudent, uninhibited, abrasive, hot-tempered and brash. Joy was fully aware of how she was perceived, but she could care less.

Additionally, Joy was a person who cared very little about her external appearance. She was usually described as frumpy or matronly.

Her Commitment to Communism

Joy's demeanor fit well with her new-found passion for Communism and its rejection of normative values. She had become a member of the party early in 1938. She always claimed that her decision to become a Communist was spurred by her compassion for the suffering masses of the Great Depression.

As is the case with most converts to anything, Joy threw herself passionately into her newly discovered secular religion. Consequently, before long, she was added to the staff of a Marxist weekly literature magazine called *New Masses.*

Her Marriage

Through her activities in the Communist Party, Joy met a writer named William (Bill) Lindsay Gresham. They started dating and ended up getting married in August of 1942 when Joy was 27 years old.

The marriage was in trouble from the start. Bill proved to be an abusive alcoholic and a serial adulterer. He never tried to cover up his extra-marital affairs, nor did he try to defend them. He simply could not see anything wrong with them.

The couple gave birth to two boys — David in 1944 and Douglas in 1945. The stress of dealing with an alcoholic, unfaithful husband and two small boys caused Joy to start drifting away from her heavy involvement in the Communist Party.

An Unexpected Conversion

The turning point for Joy came in 1946 at age 31 when she came to the end of herself. She felt completely defeated and emotionally depleted. In the midst of this personal crisis, she had a spiritual experience which she described as follows:[2]

> . . . for the first time my pride was forced to admit that I was not, after all, "the master of my fate" and "the captain of my soul." All the defenses — the walls of arrogance and cock-sureness and self-love behind which I had hid from God — went down momentarily — and God came in.

She suddenly found herself on her knees in prayer and confessed, "I must say I was the world's most surprised Atheist."[3] Amazingly, she had almost instantaneously made the transition from Atheism to Theism. But that did not make her a Christian. She still had a long way yet to go.

Discovering C. S. Lewis

She immediately began to search for some way to manifest her newly found belief in God. She went to a Presbyterian church where she was baptized. But it was only a religious rite that she felt she ought to do as a manifestation of her rejection of Atheism.

Proof of this is the fact that she soon stumbled across L. Ron Hubbard's book, *Dianetics*, which was published in 1950. The book claimed to be a manual for mental health, but Hubbard very quickly developed his teachings into a religious cult called Scientology. Both Joy and her husband became practitioners and teachers of Dianetics.

But Joy kept searching, and when she realized that Hubbard was converting his fans into a cultic group, she started pulling away from Scientology and began reading

Christian writings.

That's when she encountered C. S. Lewis, who had been featured on the cover of *Time* magazine in 1947 as one of Christendom's foremost defenders of the faith. Lewis at that time was a renowned lecturer of Medieval Literature at Oxford University in England.

In January of 1950, when Joy was 35 years old, she wrote her first letter to Lewis. It was full of theological questions. Lewis had never heard of her, but he was deeply impressed by her intellect and erudition — also her humor. He responded in depth to her questions, and they soon became "pen-friends."

Meanwhile, her husband had become so out of control that Joy felt the need to separate from him for a while and seek counsel. She decided to go to England to meet her "pen-friend" and seek his insights. She arranged for a cousin of hers to keep her children and look after Bill, and she departed for England in August 1952. She had arranged to stay with another of her pen-pals — a lady in London.

Meeting Lewis

Upon arrival, she contacted Lewis and invited him to have lunch with her and her friend. Lewis accepted the invitation and brought his brother Warren (called Warnie), with him. Both Lewis and his brother (who lived together) found Joy to be "enthralling," and Warren noted in his diary that she kept Jack (as Lewis' family and friends always called him) "laughing uproariously."[4] Additional luncheon meetings finally led to an invitation for Joy to spend a fortnight (two weeks) with Lewis and his brother before her return to the States. This period of time included Christmas of 1952.

During her time at the Lewis household, Joy read the manuscript of a book on prayer that Jack was writing, and she made suggestions for improving it. In return, Jack gave her suggestions for editing the book she was working on called *Smoke on the Mountain*, which was her commentary on the Ten Commandments.

Another Family Crisis

Before Joy departed for the States, she received a letter from her husband in which he informed her that he had fallen in love with her cousin, and they had decided to get married. He asked Joy for a divorce. Joy shared the letter with Jack and asked for his advice. He strongly advised her to divorce Bill because of his infidelity.

When Joy returned home in January of 1953, Bill was drunk. He beat her up and choked her. That was the last straw for her. She decided to return to England with her sons. Bill proceeded to divorce her and marry her cousin.

Her Return to England

Joy arrived back in England in November 1953. She rented an apartment, put her boys in boarding school, and set about to revive her relationship with the Lewis brothers. Jack and Warnie continued to be enthralled with her. But Jack's professor friends were not the least bit impressed. They considered her to be a typical "ugly American" — pushy, abrasive, over-bearing and vulgar.

She and Jack began to see each other regularly. They would take long walks together, debate theology and discuss English literature. Jack was 55 years old at the time, 17 years older than Joy.

Joy filled a void in Jack's life. Despite all her overwhelming faults, he deeply enjoyed her profound intellect and he fell in love with her mind. Gradually, he began to fall in love with her emotionally. Nor was she the only one he cherished. That's because Jack had become very attached to her two sons who were 12 and 13.

A Legal Crisis

In 1956, another crisis arose in Joy's life when the British Foreign Office informed her that they were not going to renew her permit to remain in England. Jack could not face the possibility of losing the trio he had grown to love so much. His response was to propose a civil marriage which would enable Joy and her boys to remain in England. The marriage took place on April 23, 1956. The act was, in effect, a naturalization process for Joy.

Jack and Joy had decided that for the time being their marriage would remain a secret. Joy continued to live at her house and Jack at his. But they visited each other frequently, and before long, rumors began to circulate. Jack decided that to avoid malicious gossip, he would seek to have their marriage blessed by the Church. But the Bishop of Oxford refused because Joy had been divorced.

A Health Crisis

Meanwhile, in June of 1956, Joy began experiencing pain in her left hip. In October, the hip suddenly gave way and she took a bad fall which produced excruciating pain. She was rushed to a hospital where it was discovered that she had cancer in her left femur and a malignant tumor in one of her breasts.

In December, as her condition grew steadily worse, Jack decided to announce their marriage in the newspaper.

By late January of 1957, it was clear that her radiation treatments were having no effect. Her pain was constant, and there were signs of imminent death. Jack asked an Anglican priest friend of his to pray for Joy's healing. He agreed.

When the priest arrived at the hospital and saw Joy's pitiful condition and learned of her desperate desire for a church wedding, he agreed to conduct the ceremony then and there. And so, Jack and Joy's marriage was consecrated by

Joy and Jack photographed during one of their frequent walks — most likely in the Summer of 1959 when he was 61 and she was 44.
(https://jackgibbons.blogspot.com)

the Church on March 21, 1957. He was 59 and she was 42.

Joy was now ready to die. The doctors gave her two months to live, at most. But, instead, she suddenly began to improve! Throughout the summer and fall, she continued to gain strength, and in January 1958, her cancer was proclaimed to be "arrested." The doctors were amazed.

Days of Happiness

She moved into Jack's house and immediately set about to remodel it inside and out — something it badly needed. As they settled into life as husband and wife, Jack began experiencing the happiest days of his life.

In the Summer of 1959 they began traveling throughout England and Ireland, but in October, exactly two years after her diagnosis, the cancer returned with a vengeance. They sensed there was little time left, so they decided to take one last trip to the place Joy had always dreamed of visiting — Greece. They went in April of 1960, and by the time they got back home, Joy was very weak. Tests revealed that the cancer had spread throughout her body.

Death

In July of 1960, at age 45, Joy had to be hospitalized again. And on the evening of July 13, with Jack at her side, she smiled and said, "I am at peace with God."[5] Thosc were her last words.

Jack later summarized his wife and their relationship with these remarkable words:[6]

> Joy was a splendid thing; a soul straight, bright and tempered like a sword. But not a perfected saint. A sinful woman married to a sinful man; two of God's patients, not yet cured.

Jack died three years later on November 23, 1963. His death went almost unnoticed because that was the day that President John F. Kennedy was assassinated.

And so you have it — the incredible story of how an

American Jewish Communist became the wife of a British professor who was Christendom's greatest defender of the faith.

Some Summary Thoughts

The life of Joy Davidman is just another example of how God can transform anyone through the power of His Holy Spirit — and how He desires to do so. The Bible says that "God does not wish that any should perish, but that all should come to repentance" (2 Peter 3:9). No matter how repulsive a person may be in his or her beliefs, personality or lifestyle, God desires for that person to come to know Jesus as Lord and Savior.

There are three other points I would like to make, and then I will draw this story to a close.

First, in 1948, Jack began writing his spiritual autobiography which he titled, *Surprised by Joy.* That was two years before he received his first letter from Joy Davidman. The title of this remarkable book, which was finally published in 1955, turned out to have a double meaning.

Yes, Jack was overwhelmed with spiritual joy when he came to know Jesus as his Lord and Savior at the age of 32. But, later, he was also impacted with mental and physical joy when Joy Davidman came into his life.

My second point relates to the remarkable parallels in the lives of Joy and Jack. Just as Joy announced at age 12 that she was an Atheist, Jack did the same thing at age 15. At age 31, Joy had a deeply spiritual experience that transformed her from an Atheist to a Theist. The same thing happened to Jack at the same age. And his description of the event sounded just like Joy's: "I gave in, and admitted that God was God, and knelt and prayed: perhaps, that night, the most dejected and reluctant convert in all England."[7] Joy did not become a Christian until two years after her conversion to Theism, and the same was true of Jack.

Spiritually they followed exactly the same path. But their personalities were as different as night and day.

My third observation relates to the powerful book that C. S. Lewis wrote in response to Joy's death. It was titled, *A Grief Observed.* The book is a daily journal of Jack's thoughts as he grieved over the loss of his wife.

A Chronicle of Grief

All of Jack's previous books related to religion had been intellectual exercises in which he applied his profound logic to theological problems. But this book was produced out of raw emotion, speaking from a broken heart.

It was published in 1961 under the pseudonym, N. W. Clerk. Its true author was not revealed until 1963 after Jack's death. It is believed that Lewis felt like the book would be too great a shock to his admirers — the reason being that the book lays bare his anger with God over Joy's death.

For example, the book begins with Lewis asking, "Where is God?"[8] He then asks another profound question: "Why is He so present a commander in our time of prosperity and so very absent a help in time of trouble?"[9]

Keep in mind that this is the foremost defender of the Christian faith who is asking these questions.

Lewis follows up these questions by quickly stating that he is not in much danger of ceasing to believe in God. "The real danger," he explains, "is of coming to believe such dreadful things about Him."[10] For example, is He truly a God of love, grace and mercy, or is He a "Cosmic Sadist"?[11] Lewis concludes this section by saying he feels like God has slammed a door in his face.

But as Jack begins to emerge from his grief, he looks back over his struggle with God and says that he can see that God was with him all along, but that God was unable to comfort him because he was like a drowning man flailing around and pushing away anyone wanting to help.[12]

At one point in the book, Jack observes that throughout his ordeal, people have been telling him, "God is testing your faith." But he concludes that they have been wrong. He writes:[13]

> God has not been trying an experiment on my faith or love in order to find out their quality. He knew it already. It was I who didn't . . . He always knew that my temple was a house of cards. His only way of making me realize that fact was to knock it down.

This book has often been characterized as a "crisis of faith." I can understand how it could be viewed that way. But in actuality, it was a demonstration of Lewis' deep faith. For throughout the book he is talking with God, not denying Him.

Like King David in his psalms, Jack was just being truthful with God. His heart was hurting, and he said so, not mincing any words. And that is what I love about David's psalms. When he hurts, he says so. When he's angry or doubtful, he says so. When he encounters joy, he cries out to God in thankfulness. He had an honest and open relationship with God.

So did C. S. Lewis. Do you?

Chapter 7

A Ruthless Political Operative

"For what is a man profited if he gains the whole world, and loses or forfeits himself?"
(Luke 9:25)

This is the story of "a broken man transformed by the love and power of Jesus Christ."[1] These are the words Chuck Colson used to introduce his autobiography, *Born Again*, published in 1976.

He continued with this observation: "It's the kind of story Christ has created in countless people's hearts for two thousand years — the story of Romans 8:28 in action, of God using *all* things for good to those who love Him and are called according to His purpose."[2]

It is the story of a loose canon nicknamed "the hatchet man" being transformed into a humble servant of Jesus.

The Early Years

The story began on October 16, 1931, with the birth in Boston, Massachusetts of Charles (Chuck) Wendell Colson. His parents were far from Boston nobility. At the end of World War I, his grandfather had died of the influenza epidemic, and Chuck's dad had to drop out of high school to help support the family.

After his dad and mom got married, his dad spent the next 12 years in night school earning degrees in accounting and law while working as a bookkeeper at a meat packing plant. When Chuck was born, his parents were living in a small walk-up apartment.

With his law degree, Chuck's dad began to experience business success as he climbed the corporate ladder at General Foods. However, he soon started experiencing poor health and had to quit his job. Thereafter, he scrambled to make ends meet as he practiced law on his own.

From these early years, Chuck inherited several things. First, his dad taught him the importance of hard work and education. Second, Chuck developed animosity toward the Harvard dominated elite law firms that cornered the legal market in Boston.

Unfortunately, Chuck received very little spiritual training during his formative years. His parents took him to an Episcopal church, but he later said, "It never made much of an impression on me."[3] At one point, however, Chuck said, that he "suddenly became as certain as I had ever been about anything in my life that out there in that great starlight beyond was God."[4] But this awareness of God did not last long. As Chuck put it, "My awareness of God faded as personal interests crowded my life."[5]

Education

Chuck worked hard at the small private prep school he attended in Cambridge. He was editor of the school newspaper, voted most likely to succeed, and graduated with honors. In fact, he was elected to give the valedictory address for his class. He was ready to take on the world.

Because of his outstanding academic record, he was offered a full academic scholarship to Harvard, which he rejected! He was fed up with the condescension of the aristocratic Harvard men toward those who came from less fortunate backgrounds.

So, Chuck enrolled in Brown University in Providence, Rhode Island and graduated from there in 1953. He then married and joined the Marines, where he served the next four years. Like his father, he attended law school at night at George Washington University, graduating in 1959. During this time, his wife bore him three children — two boys and a girl. The marriage lasted 11 years, until 1964. After the divorce, Chuck married again in the same year.

The Plunge Into Politics

Chuck began his serious participation in politics during the Presidential election of 1960. John F. Kennedy was the Democratic nominee who was expected to carry his home state of Massachusetts overwhelmingly.

A Massachusetts Senator, Leverett Saltonstall, a Republican, was up for re-election and appeared to have little hope. The Senator hired Chuck to do some election wizardry that would tie him to the coattails of Kennedy. By that time, Chuck had gotten a street education in the dirty politics of Boston. Here's how Chuck put it:[6]

> I had learned all the tricks, some of which went up to and even slightly over the legal boundaries. Phony mailings, tearing down opposition signs, planting misleading stories in the press, voting tombstones and spying out the opposition in every possible way were all standard fare.

To everyone's surprise, Saltonstall was re-elected. Following the election, Chuck established his own law firm which grew rapidly, with offices in Boston and Washington, D.C.

Richard Nixon

Chuck first met Richard Nixon when he was Vice President. He impressed Chuck as being a man of "immense intellect." He was also struck by things they had in common:[7]

> Nixon and I understood each other — a young, ambitious political kingmaker and an

> older pretender to the throne. We were both men of the same lower middle class origins, men who'd known hard work all our lives, prideful men seeking that most elusive goal — acceptance and respect . . .

After Kennedy's victory in 1960, Chuck presented Nixon with a long memo describing how he could make a political comeback. But when 1964 arrived, Senator Barry Goldwater had the Republican nomination sewed up. Nonetheless, Nixon was greatly impressed with Chuck's analysis as a political strategist.

Later, during Nixon's 1968 campaign against Senator Hubert Humphrey, Chuck served as a counsel to Nixon's Key Issues Committee. Again, he greatly impressed Nixon with his realistic, political savvy.

The call to serve Nixon finally came in the Fall of 1969. Nixon asked Chuck to serve as his White House Counsel — a very high honor — and Chuck agreed. He was only 38 years old, and he had reached the pinnacle of success.

Serving Nixon

Chuck very quickly developed a reputation as Nixon's "hit man." Chuck himself admitted that he was a "loose cannon," willing to do anything for the President.[8] Chuck was, in fact, very proud of his notorious reputation. He bragged about the slogan affixed to the wall of his den which said, "When you've got'em by the balls, their hearts and minds will follow."[9]

Eager to demonstrate his loyalty to Nixon, Chuck confirmed that a quote of his in a staff memo that was leaked to the press was true: "I would be willing to walk over my grandmother for Nixon."[10] Looking back on this time later in life, Chuck observed: "I was willing at times to blink at certain ethical standards, to be ruthless in getting things done.

It was earning status and power for me."[11]

The task Chuck performed for Nixon that would ultimately lead to his downfall was an attempt to blacken the reputation of a former Pentagon official, Daniel Ellsberg, who was suspected of leaking secret Defense Department papers that revealed U.S. strategy for the Vietnam War.

Nixon ordered Chuck to "use any means" to stop Ellsberg. In his autobiography, Chuck said that this order was when the Nixon Administration crossed the Rubicon, descending into illegal activities.[12]

Chuck recruited an ex-CIA agent named Howard Hunt to put together a team of burglars. Hunt recruited an ex-FBI agent, Gordon Liddy. They, in turn recruited a group of Cubans to assist them. This team, known as "the plumbers," proceeded to break into the office of a Los Angeles psychiatrist in September of 1971. They were seeking damning information about Ellsberg who was a former patient of the doctor.

This was the same team that was later caught while burglarizing the Watergate offices of the Democratic Party in Washington, D.C. in June of 1972. However, Chuck was not directly involved in this affair, even though he ultimately became the poster boy for the Watergate scandal.

Because the press focused on Chuck, he decided to resign as the President's Special Counsel. This he did in March of 1973, following Nixon's re-election in 1972. One year later, Chuck was indicted for obstruction of justice for his efforts to cover-up the burglaries.

The Turning Point

During the year between his resignation and his indictment, Chuck's life had changed radically. It all began with a meeting he had with one his law firm's top clients, Tom Phillips, who was the CEO of Raytheon.

Charles W. Colson
(Nixon Presidential Library)

Tom sensed that Chuck was distraught, so he recommended that he lean on Jesus. Chuck was shocked. This was not the hard-driving ruthless businessman he had previously known, and Tom's recommendation of Jesus astounded Chuck. Tom then explained that he had recently accepted Jesus as his Savior and had committed his life to Him. Here's how Chuck described his response:[13]

> If I hadn't restrained myself, I would have blurted out, "What are you talking about? Jesus Christ lived two thousand years ago — a great moral leader, of course, and doubtless divinely inspired. But why would I 'accept' Him or 'commit my life to Him' as if He were still around today?"

This encounter shook Chuck's soul. He realized he was living an empty life with an "inner malaise."[14] Chuck was startled again in an interview with Mike Wallace on *60 Minutes* when he was asked about the morality of working for a White House that was engaged in intimidation and smear campaigns. The shock came when Wallace followed up this observation by asking, "Are you truly living up to your Christian beliefs?"[15]

This led to a second meeting with Tom Phillips who emphasized to Chuck that Jesus was more than just a historical figure — that He was God in the flesh and was alive today. As they parted, Tom gave Chuck a copy of C. S. Lewis' book, *Mere Christianity*. He told him to read it and to get in touch with some Christians in the D.C. area who could help him grow in the Lord.

Lewis' book had a profound impact on Chuck. He wrote: "I opened *Mere Christianity* and found myself face-to-face with an intellect so disciplined, so lucid, so relentlessly logical that I could only be grateful I had never faced him in a court of law."[16]

Chuck was particularly impressed with Lewis' reasoning that Jesus had to be God or a lunatic! He could not get this point out of his mind. He studied Lewis' arguments for a week, and then one morning, "words I had not been certain I could understand or say fell naturally from my lips: 'Lord Jesus, I believe in You. I accept You. Please come into my life. I commit to You.'"[17]

The Aftermath

One of the first things Chuck did afer his conversion — over the objections of his family and defense lawyers — was to go to the prosecutors and offer them evidence that would enable them to convict him so that he could pay the penalty for his crimes.

He was convicted and given a sentence of one to three years. He was also disbarred. He spent seven months in prison, being released in January of 1975. During his time in prison, he became convinced that God was calling him to do something about the many legal injustices he witnessed.

So, in 1976, Chuck founded a ministry called Prison Fellowship which quickly became the nation's largest Christian outreach to prisoners. This ministry went international in 1979 and now exists in 120 nations around the world.

Chuck also became an outspoken critic of postmodernism and used a variety of media channels to express a biblical viewpoint on contemporary societal issues. He often argued that a society without a Christian foundation could not long survive.[18]

Chuck received many honorary doctorates, and in 1993 he was given the one million dollar Templeton Prize for Progress in Religion, which he donated to his ministry. His highest earthly reward came in 2008 when President George W. Bush presented him with the Presidential Citizen's Medal.

On April 21, 2012, at age 80, Chuck was called home to his Heavenly award. He died from complications resulting from a brain hemorrhage.

Conclusion

Once again, through the life of Chuck Colson, God revealed the incredible life-changing power of Jesus. And Chuck devoted the rest of his life focusing his ministry on transferring that life-changing experience to people in prison who desperately needed a new start in life.

He did so by sharing with them the good news of Jesus and by encouraging them to receive Jesus as their Lord and Savior, proving over and over again that Jesus is the only sure cure to recidivism.

Chapter 8

A Popular Movie Star

1 John 2

15) Do not love the world nor the things in the world. If anyone loves the world, the love of the Father is not in him.

16) For all that is in the world, the lust of the flesh and the lust of the eyes and the boastful pride of life, is not from the Father, but is from the world.

I first became acquainted with Steve McQueen on Christmas Day in 1968. My brother, sister and their families joined mine at our parent's house in Waco, Texas to celebrate Christmas. We opened our presents on Christmas morning, followed by feasting on a huge Thanksgiving-style lunch.

My father then announced that he wanted to see the hottest Hollywood movie being shown at the time — a film titled, *Bullitt*, starring Steve McQueen.[1] He asked my brother and me to accompany him.

The film was about a San Francisco police detective named Frank Bullitt, the role that McQueen played.

The movie had become an overnight sensation, mainly because of three sensational chase scenes contained in it. The first occurs at the beginning of the film and follows Bullitt chasing a criminal from the top floor of a hospital to the basement. The film ends with another chase sequence, with Bullitt pursuing a criminal at night back and forth across runways at San Francisco International Airport as planes are

(https://www.pinterest.com)

taking off and landing.

But the BIG chase scene that people were clamoring to see was a spectacular car chase in the middle of the film that runs for 11 minutes as Bullitt chases two criminals up and down the steep streets of San Francisco.

A Big Surprise

So, my dad and brother and I settled into our seats that Christmas afternoon, anxious to witness the longest and most dangerous car chase in movie history. But, believe it or not, the moment the car chase began, the movie image suddenly shifted from the screen to the ceiling and stayed there for the entire race! The audience went berserk. People were screaming and cursing.

Being Christmas Day, we assumed the projectionist was probably a substitute and that he had failed to lock down the projector securely while he went to the bathroom — but we never knew for sure.

The problem caused chaos at the box office because about half the audience decided to stay and see the movie again, making it impossible for most of the people standing in line outside to enter the theater.

Steve McQueen in 1968

In this film, Steve McQueen played a detective who was a loner and who was cocky, belligerent, rebellious and insubordinate — a true maverick. McQueen was perfectly cast because he was simply playing himself.

By this time in his career, McQueen had reached the pinnacle of success. He had become one of the leading male stars of Hollywood. He was known as "The King of Cool."

Unfortunately, he had also become a classic Hollywood ego-maniac, and that made him difficult to get along with. He tried to take over every film he made, telling the director how to direct, rewriting the scripts and stealing scenes from his fellow cast members. He had also reached the stage in his career when he could demand enormous salaries plus a percentage of the profits. All this he did with a belligerent attitude that turned people off.

McQueen's Early Life

Steve McQueen was born in March of 1930 in Beach Grove, Indiana, a suburb of Indianapolis. He was the product of a one-night stand. His father was a philandering stunt pilot, and his mother was a teenage alcoholic prostitute.[2] His father abandoned Steve and his mom six months after his son's birth.

His mom was unable to care for Steve, so she unloaded him on a wealthy uncle who lived in Missouri. But it wasn't long before she returned for Steve and took him to Los Angeles where she had remarried.

Her new husband proved to be very abusive to Steve, so he ran away from home and started living on the streets. He joined a gang that focused on burglarizing small businesses. He was only 13 at the time!

Steve was sent back to live with his uncle. But at age 14, he joined a traveling circus that eventually ended up back in L.A. where he reconnected with his mom and got involved again in gangs. He got into so much trouble that he was sent to a reform school in Chino, California, called "The California Junior Boy's Republic." He was 15.

Fortunately, the school was a very progressive one where the boys were treated with respect as human beings rather than simply as prisoners. Steve appreciated his treatment and became a lifelong supporter of the school, benefitting it with donations and personal appearances to encourage the boys.

While Steve was confined to Boy's Republic, his mother moved to New York City, so when he was released in 1946 from his 14 month term, he headed immediately to New York, only to discover that his mom wanted nothing to do with him.

Steve's Adult Life

Steve ran through a plethora of jobs before deciding to join the Marines. His three-year enlistment was stormy from beginning to end. He quickly earned a reputation as a trouble maker. He constantly had run-ins with officers and spent considerable time in the brig for going AWOL.

As soon as he got out of the Marines, Steve headed back to New York to take up residence in the artsy area of Greenwich Village. Again, he worked a variety of jobs as a taxi driver, auto mechanic, waiter and dishwasher. He even resorted to shoplifting to make ends meet.

Finally, a girl friend suggested that he try acting. The idea immediately appealed to Steve because he wanted to escape from manual labor. He used the GI Bill of Rights to finance his training in Method Acting. After his graduation, he started living the life of endless auditions, mainly for TV shows. Later in life, Steve said that if he had not pursued a career in acting, he probably would have ended up living a life of crime.[3]

Steve knocked around New York for several years performing roles in stage plays, TV programs and a few cheap movies. His big break came in 1958 when he was given the

Steve McQueen
(www.alamy.com)

starring role as a bounty hunter in a Western TV series called, "Wanted Dead or Alive." The program was an immediate success. Steve was 28.

Steve's Marriages

Meanwhile, Steve had gotten married for the first time in 1956 to an actor and dancer from the Philippines named Neile. By this time, Steve had already developed a reputation for being a wanton womanizer.

Neile was fully aware of this, but she seemed to take the attitude that such a lifestyle was inevitable for those in the art world. She just put up with Steve's infidelities for 15 years, until 1972, bearing him two children during that time — a daughter and a son.

Steve's second marriage resulted from a torrid affair he had with actress Ali McGraw in 1972 while making the movie *The Getaway*. They were married in 1973 and divorced in 1977. Ali could not tolerate Steve's womanizing.

By the time of the divorce, Steve was already living with another woman — a beautiful model named Barbara Minty. They would remain together for the next three years, until Steve's death in 1980. They actually married in January 1980, 11 months before Steve died in November.

A Major Decision

A strange thing happened in Steve's life in 1974 after the release of his film called *The Towering Inferno*. Steve decided to retire from the movies! He was at the top of his career, rated as the number one male actor in Hollywood. *The Towering Inferno* had been a smash hit. Steve netted ten percent of the film's $35 million. He was Hollywood's highest paid actor.

But Steve's personal life was in the toilet. His second marriage had gone down the drain. He was addicted to alcohol, drugs, fast cars and faster women. He was also a compulsive spender. He had amassed huge collections of antique cars, guns and motorcycles.

In sum, Steve had all the world had to offer — money and worldwide fame — but he felt empty. So, he retreated into himself and began to reassess his life.

The only reason he made three additional movies is because he was confronted with a contract he had signed years ago to make a certain number of films for a movie studio, and he had not fulfilled the contract.

So, he knocked off three movies in 1978 and '79. All three were bombs. One was so awful that it was never released. In short, he walked through them just to get them out of the way. It was clear that he was fed up with movie-making.

At this point in his life, Steve reminded me of King

Solomon. Like Steve, he was a very talented man who ended up enormously rich. Also like Steve, Solomon became enamored with women. And like Steve, he became obsessed with money and the use of it to amass collections of things — for Solomon it was horses. Yet, at the end of his life, Solomon looked back, at his hedonistic, materialistic lifestyle and declared it to be "vanity." He then declared, "Here now is my final conclusion: fear God and obey His commands, for this is everyone's duty" (Ecclesiastes 12:13 - NLT).

As Steve reassessed his life, it must have occurred to him that he had achieved all his goals. He had conquered the movie world. He had more money than he knew what to do with. He had sought meaning in alcohol, drugs, sex and the amassing of huge collections of material things. And now that he had accomplished all this, he felt empty. He sensed that he had not found the true meaning of life.

Seeking Privacy

It was at this point that Steve and Barbara retreated to a small rural village called Santa Paula, located about 65 miles northwest of L.A. They settled on 15 acres of land containing a farm house that was built in 1896.

Steve decided to purchase a biplane and learn how to fly. He had a renowned pilot to instruct him. His name was Sammy Mason. He was in his early 60s. Steve was in his late 40s.

Steve was not aware that Sammy was a devout Christian who was also very evangelistic. Sammy decided that every moment he was in the air with Steve, he would share with him the Gospel and the importance of having a personal relationship with Jesus.

The story of Steve's remarkable conversion to Jesus that subsequently occurred is presented in detail in a book by Grady Ragsdale, Jr., titled, *Steve McQueen: The Final Chap-*

ter.[4] The author was Steve's closest friend at the end of his life.

Steve' Conversion

Steve and Barbara began attending church services at the Ventura Missionary Church. They also started having a daily devotional time when they would read the Bible and pray. Steve's buddy, Grady, was overwhelmed by the changes he observed in Steve:[5]

> From that moment on, I saw a dramatic change in Steve. I had always felt that he possessed a depth of character, but when Christ infiltrated his life and brought it in line with God's will, the full beauty of the man began to blossom. Oh, he still had problems with his quick temper and with areas of his life that had been poorly cultivated for many years, but I doubt that I have ever seen a man flourish with more spiritual reality in such a short time.

When Grady remarked to Steve how astonished he was with the changes taking place in his life, Steve responded by saying, "The Lord's rearranging my life to be more upright."[6]

The pastor of the church where Steve and Barbara were attending also noticed the change in Steve's life and attitude. One Sunday after church, the pastor asked them to have lunch with him.

The pastor later reported that he told Steve, "I have one question for you." But before he could pose the question, Steve said, "You want to know if I have become a born-again Christian." The pastor replied, "That's right," and Steve responded, "Yes, I have asked Jesus Christ to take over my life."[7]

The Final Days

It was six months later, in December 1979, that Steve decided to have a medical checkup. He had developed a cough he could not get rid of. The test results were shocking. They revealed that he had a form of terminal lung cancer called mesothelioma — a rare form of cancer caused by inhaling asbestos fibers.

Steve linked the cancer to a six-week period in the Marines when he was required to clean an engine room where all the pipes were insulated with asbestos. He remembered the air being full of asbestos particles.

The first thing Steve did in response to the diagnosis was to marry Barbara in January 1980. They were married by their pastor in the living room of their ranch house.

Steve followed that up by trying to get in touch with Billy Graham. Over the next few months, Billy tried to arrange his schedule to meet with Steve, but it proved very difficult because Steve started making frequent trips to Mexico where he was being treated by a holistic doctor.

Finally, in November of 1980, the meeting with Graham was arranged at Steve's ranch house. Graham later reported that Steve told him that months before his diagnosis, he had accepted Christ as his Savior. Graham said he found Steve "happy and totally at peace."[8] They read some scriptures together and then prayed.

Graham rode with Steve back to the airport in L.A. where Steve boarded a plane for Mexico. He was scheduled to have surgery to remove some tumors. After boarding the plane, Graham prayed with Steve once more and gave him a Bible. It was inscribed: "To my friend, Steve McQueen. May God bless you and keep you always. Billy Graham. Philippians 1:6, November 2, 1980."

The verse that Graham referred to reads as follows: "For I am confident of this very thing, that He who began a good work in you will perfect it until the day of Christ Jesus."

Five days later, on November 7, Steve died in Juarez, Mexico of a heart attack after surgery. He died holding Graham's Bible. He was 50 years old.

Some of Steve's last words to his dear friend, Grady, were: "I expect to win this battle, but no matter how it goes, I'm at peace with God. I can't lose."[9]

The "King of Cool" had at long last submitted himself to the King of kings.

Contemporary Examples

Chapter 9

A Fortune 500 Executive

John 8

31) So, Jesus was saying . . . "If you abide in
My word, then you are truly My disciples;

32) and you will know the truth, and the truth
will make you free."

(Mike Gendron and his wife, Jane, live in the Dallas-Ft. Worth area. He is the founder and spokesman of a ministry called Proclaiming the Gospel.)

My life began in 1947 at Ft. Banning, Georgia where I was born into a devout Roman Catholic family with three brothers and a sister. My dad was an Army Colonel and his bother was a Catholic priest. Our family lived and traveled throughout the world, including three years in Naples, Italy, and seven months in Rangoon, Burma.

I was indoctrinated very early into the traditions of the Catholic faith to the point where I was convinced the Catholic Church was the one true church. I thought I was so "lucky" to have been baptized a Catholic.

It was my privilege to become an altar boy and learn Latin to serve the priests during the sacrifice of the Mass. Since I was always seeking to earn merit before God, I earned the Catholic "Ad Altar Dei Award," which was the highest religious award in the Boy Scouts. Later I earned the highest rank in Scouting — Eagle Scout.

But the highlight of my early life was to serve Mass with

the Catholic Saint, Padre Pio (1887-1968), alongside my uncle, Father Charles Gendron, in San Giovanni Rotondo, Italy. Padre Pio's body was marked with the stigmata, which according to Catholic teaching, represent the wounds of Jesus Christ during His crucifixion. As a young Catholic, this was convincing proof to me that the Catholic Church was the true church founded by Christ.

My college years were spent in the heavily Catholic area of southern Louisiana where I pursued a degree in Mathematics while playing baseball for the University of Southwestern Louisiana's "Ragin' Cajuns."

Upon graduation in 1970, I went to work for NASA at Cape Kennedy, Florida in the space program, working as a mathematician. In 1974, I moved to Dallas, Texas, to work for Ross Perot at Electronic Data Systems.

A Dedicated Catholic

As a committed Catholic, I attended St. Anthony's Catholic Church in Dallas, and I taught High School CCD (Confraternity of Christian Doctrine). Later in 1981, I was responsible for helping to start the first *Little Rock Scripture Study* in Texas at St. Patrick's Catholic Church in Dallas.

Up until that time I had never read the Bible because the priests told me it was too difficult to understand. They told me if I had questions they would answer them for me.

Shortly after I began reading and studying the Bible, I had a crisis of faith. The plan of salvation that I was reading in God's Word was diametrically opposed to the plan of salvation that I was taught as a Catholic. With very little knowledge of God's Word, I knew enough to realize "there is a way which seems right to a man, but its end is the way of death" (Proverbs 14:12).

Little did I know that this was the beginning of my spiritual journey from darkness to light. I called my uncle the priest and asked him why the Catholic plan of salvation was different from the biblical plan. I quoted Ephesians 2:8-9 which says, "For by grace you have been saved through faith, and this not of yourselves, it is the gift of God."

My uncle told me that God does not really mean what He is saying there! So I kept studying God's Word and soon realized there was no way to reconcile Catholic teaching about salvation with the Scriptures.

A Crisis of Faith

My crisis of faith boiled down to making a choice between believing the inspired Word of God or the uninspired words of men. It was impossible to believe both. I read that Jesus was the truth, that His Word is truth and that He came to testify to the truth (John 14:6; 17:17; 18:37).

I believe this is when God opened my eyes to see the light of the Gospel and the glory of Christ. It was the Word of God illuminated by the Spirit of God that caused me to become alive in Christ. I turned from believing priests and popes to believing Christ and His Word. God called me to Himself through His Gospel which is "the power of God for salvation to everyone who believes" (Romans 1:16). I was 35 years old at the time.

Life Without Christ

Looking back on my 35 years of living in spiritual darkness and my subsequent 42 years of walking in the light with Christ, I chose four words that characterize each of those periods of time. My life without Christ can be described by the words: Worldly, Enslaved, Religious and Deceived.

My Life Without Christ Was Worldly

From the world's perspective my first 35 years were remarkably successful. I excelled in athletics, playing baseball all the way through college, and winning a gold medal in springboard diving.

After earning an MBA at the University of Texas at Dallas, I channeled all my competitive energy into a rapid climb to the top of the corporate ladder. My success in business led to my becoming the National Sales Manager for Apex Corporation, a Fortune 500 company.

All this success in the business world enabled me to acquire wealth and recognition but it also led me into a hedonistic, pleasure-seeking lifestyle. I was corrupted by deceitful desires and had given myself over to sensuality, with a continual lust for more (Ephesians 4:19).

I built my lavish dream house in one of the most esteemed neighborhoods in Dallas, joined a prestigious country club and purchased a Mercedes 380 SL sports car and a gold Rolex watch, the universal sign of accomplishment.

Yet with all this success and wealth, there was still a nagging void in my life. "For all that is in the world, the lust of the flesh and the lust of the eyes and the boastful pride of life, is not from the Father, but is from the world" (1 John 2:16).

My Life Without Christ Was Enslaved

My enslavement was all encompassing and I was powerless to do anything about it. Not only was I in bondage to sin but also to the legalism of Catholic traditions (Colossians 2:8).

The Catholic priests, like Judaizers in the time of Christ, were false brethren who kept me in bondage (Galatians 2:4). Their confessional box was a place I dreaded to go. Each week I had to confess the same sins to the same priest because I was disobedient, deceived and enslaved to various lusts and pleasures (Titus 3:3).

Many times, I would disguise my voice so the priest wouldn't know it was me again. Undeniably, I was ensnared by the devil and held captive by him to do his will (2 Timothy

2:26).

My Life Without Christ Was Religious

As a Catholic, I faithfully participated in religious rituals and received the sacraments to merit God's grace and to avoid the fires of Hell. In retrospect, I was motivated more by a fear of Hell than a desire to be with God. All my religious activity gave me an external righteousness that covered my corrupt and depraved nature.

Yet according to Isaiah, all my righteous acts were like filthy rags (64:6). I had a zeal for God, but it wasn't based on biblical knowledge. So, I sought to establish my own righteousness before God (Romans 10:3). Now I know how Satan destroys religious people for their lack of knowledge (Hosea 4:6).

My Life Without Christ Was Deceived

I had no way to discern truth from error because I was biblically ignorant. It wasn't that I didn't have a Bible. In fact, I had a huge one displayed in my home as a sign of piety. I never bothered to read it because, again, the priests told me it was too difficult to understand. No one ever told me the Bible sets forth the truth plainly to every man's conscience (2 Corinthians 4:2).

Because of my lack of biblical knowledge I was easily deceived. I lived in error because I did not know the Scriptures or the power of God (Matthew 22:29). Satan, who deceives the whole world had blinded me from the truth of the Gospel (Revelation 12:9 and 2 Corinthians 4:4). I was separated from the life of God because of the ignorance that was in me (Ephesians 4:18).

My Life With Jesus

My life with Jesus can be described by the following words: Liberated, Forgiven, Reconciled and Secured.

My Life With Jesus Was Liberated

In 1981, the Bible became my supreme authority in all matters of faith. From that point on I began trusting in the inspired Words of God, not the uninspired words of men. I began searching for answers to questions that priests were unable to explain.

I was amazed at how often the Bible contradicts Catholic teaching and tradition. The truth of God's Word began to set me free from the legalistic bondage of the Catholic Church. I read where Jesus came "to release the captives, and to set free those who are downtrodden" (Luke 4:18). He said: "If you abide in My word, then you are truly disciples of Mine; and you shall know the truth, and the truth shall make you free" (John 8:31-32).

The ransom payment for delivering sinners from the bondage of sin was the precious blood of Jesus. "He gave Himself for us, that He might redeem us from every lawless deed and purify for Himself a people for His own possession, zealous for good deeds" (Titus 2:14). It is through the power of the Holy Spirit that I can put to death the evil deeds of the flesh (Romans 8:13). The battle between my sin nature and the indwelling power of the Holy Spirit is ever present within me, but by God's grace, sin no longer is master over me. Thanks be to God that, though "I was a slave of sin, by His power He made me a slave of righteousness" (Romans 6: 17-18).

My Life With Jesus Was Forgiven

As a Catholic, each time I confessed my sins to a priest he told me I was forgiven. But was I really? I never even knew what God's forgiveness meant or what God's justice demanded as punishment for sin. Each time I entered the Catholic Church, I saw Jesus hanging on a cross but I never knew why He had to die. I never knew, that is, until I read in the Bible that the penalty for sin is death — eternal separation from God in the lake of fire (Romans 6:23, Revelation 20:14). The sin debt that must be paid to satisfy God's justice is death. Then I discovered "to forgive" means "to cancel a debt that is owed." So when God forgives a sinner He cancels the entire debt for all their sins — past, present and future. My substitute, Jesus Christ cancelled the certificate of debt against me. It was nailed to the cross (Colossians 2:14). Jesus suffered and died so that I could live. He was pierced for my transgressions. He was crushed for my iniquities (Isaiah 53:5).

Oh, how can it be that my God and Creator should die for me? The answer is profoundly given in one word — love. "God demonstrates His own love toward us, in that while we were yet sinners, Christ died for us" (Romans 5:8). My sin, not in part but the whole, was nailed to the cross. I bear it no more! "God made Him who knew no sin to be sin on my behalf, so that I might become the righteousness of God in Him" (2 Corinthians 5:21).

This was the greatest news I had ever heard! No longer was I condemned to death. Now I was justified to life! Forever! I was acquitted because God, the righteous judge, saw that divine justice was satisfied in His Only Son. "Jesus abolished death and brought life and immortality to light through the Gospel" (2 Timothy 1:10) "Through His name, everyone who believes in Him receives forgiveness of sins" (Acts 10:43).

My Life With Jesus Was Reconciled

Once I knew I had been reconciled to God through the death of His Son, I no longer needed priests offering sacrifices for my sins. "For by one offering Jesus has perfected for all time those who are sanctified" (Hebrews 10:14). No longer is there a sin barrier separating me from God (Isaiah 59:2). Jesus has given me access to the Father (Ephesians 2:18).

This was powerfully demonstrated at His death when the four-inch temple veil, separating man and his sin from God, was torn open from top to bottom. "Christ died for sins once for all, the just for the unjust, in order that He might bring us to God" (1 Peter 3:18).

Those who trust the redeeming work of Christ can exchange their religion for a relationship with almighty God. Through the blood of His cross Jesus is able to present me before God holy and blameless (Colossians 1:20-22). Jesus changed my relationship with God from one of enmity and hostility to one of peace and harmony.

My Life With Jesus Was Secured

Each time I got on an airplane as a Catholic I experienced a nagging fear concerning where I would spend eternity if the plane went down. I never knew if my sins were serious enough to warrant Hell or if I had done enough good works to qualify for Heaven.

Now as a true Christian, I know eternal life is not determined by what I do for God but by what God has done for me in Christ. I no longer have to wonder about my eternal destiny. It is based on the unconditional faithfulness of God. I am secure in Christ, and nothing I do will ever change God's promises to me. Jesus promised that He will lose no one the Father has given Him. He said, "For this is the will of My Father, that everyone who sees the Son and believes in Him, will have eternal life; and I Myself will raise him up on the last day" (John 6:40).

I came to realize that eternal life, by its very nature, can never be terminated. I am held securely in the hands of the Father and the Son, and no one can snatch me away (John 10:27-30). Those whom God justifies He also glorifies (Romans 8:30). The Holy Spirit, who is given as a pledge of our inheritance, seals everyone who hears and believes the Gospel of salvation in Christ (Ephesians 1:13-14). Based on

God's promises, I am more confident of spending eternity in Heaven than one more day on earth.

I am forever thankful that God has made me alive in Christ, healed my spiritual blindness, adopted me into His eternal family and given me the royal privilege of being an ambassador for Christ to tell others about His amazing grace! The life I live, I now live for Him!

Marriage

In 1984 while I was still working in the corporate world, I met a beautiful young lady from Albuquerque, NM, who came in for a job interview. She had a good resume of success in sales and marketing but had no experience in technology, so I could not hire her.

However, I was very interested in pursuing a relationship with her. So, I invited her to a baseball game to watch the Texas Rangers play the Boston Red Sox. After a wonderful evening of getting to know each other, she flew back to Albuquerque.

In the providence of God we continued our romantic

Mike and Jane Gendron

courtship for three exciting months until we were married in November. Little did we know at the time that her upbringing as a Roman Catholic would be a valuable asset to a ministry God was preparing for us.

A New Purpose for Living

In 1988 my love for Christ and His Word led me to enroll at Dallas Theological Seminary (DTS). I not only wanted to study God's inspired Word, but I also wanted to purge my mind of all the false teachings and traditions I had embraced as a Catholic.

During my last semester at DTS, my love and compassion for Catholics began to increase significantly. I approached my wife Jane, with a plan to share the Gospel with Catholics. We began inviting Catholics to our home every Tuesday evening to share a Gospel video that featured testimonies from former priests and nuns. Within three months we saw 17 Catholics exchange their religion for an eternal relationship with our Lord Jesus Christ.

Then we began inviting the new converts back on Wednesday nights to disciple them in God's Word and help them mature in their new life with Christ.

Our Sovereign Lord began building a ministry around our desire to see Catholics saved. Churches began inviting me to equip their congregations to encourage the saints to be effective witnesses to Roman Catholics. Then, seminaries began inviting me to preach at their Chapel services. Missionary organizations also asked me to train their missionaries to reach Catholics throughout the world. Also, my wife Jane and I have had the privilege of going on short-term mission trips to countries with large Catholic populations.

Summary

We stand in awe of what our Sovereign Lord has accomplished through a couple of broken vessels that made themselves available to work in the fields white for harvest. It has now been 33 years that I have had the privilege to direct the ministry of Proclaiming the Gospel.

As an ambassador for Christ, I have preached throughout the world including seminaries, churches and conferences. And for 20 years, I have had the privilege of preaching at The Masters Seminary Chapel and The Masters Academy International.

A significant part of my ministry to Catholics has been to produce effective resources to train and equip others to reach lost souls who are on the wide road to destruction. That was the motivation for my first book, *Preparing for Eternity*, which has served two purposes.[1] It not only equips Christians to be effective witnesses to Catholics, but also gives Catholics a powerful contrast between the inspired Word of God and their Catechism. Over the years this book has set many Catholics free from the bondage of religious deception.

My second book, *Contending for the Gospel*, is a urgent call for all Christians to contend for the purity and exclusivity of the Gospel.[2]

I am a firm believer that after we give the Gospel verbally, we should leave it in written form. This was the motivation to write and produce eight different Gospel tracts that have now been translated into multiple languages.[3]

Conclusion

There are times when I wish God had saved me earlier so I would not have wasted 35 years of my life. But now I realize that my life as a devout Catholic prepared me for the ministry that God entrusted to me. My life as a Catholic gave me a fervent compassion for those who are where I was — believing my religion would get me to Heaven when, in fact, I was destined for the eternal fires of Hell.

I have learned that the nature of deception is such that

people do not know they are deceived until they are confronted with the truth. God has given me such a passion for His truth that I want to share it with those who are deceived and don't even know it.

I encourage everyone to live with an eternal perspective to glorify our great God and Savior through His Gospel. Let us be mindful of the shortness of time, the nearness of death, the duration of eternity, the doom of lost sinners and the joy of being with our Creator forever.

We need to live with a sense of urgency and use our gifts and resources to be faithful to our Lord's Great Commission (Mark 16:15-18). The Gospel is not only a message to believe, but an invitation to receive and a command to obey!

Chapter 10

An Alcoholic

"Don't be drunk with wine,
because that will ruin your life.
Instead, be filled with the Holy Spirit."
(Ephesians 5:18 – NLT)

(Gary Sims and his wife, Cathy, live in Kentucky where he operates an insurance business. They are very active in a variety of church functions.)

I was born to a Christian family, and started going to church as a crib baby in the nursery at First Baptist church in Lawrenceburg, Kentucky. I continued to go with my parents every Sunday, and I accepted Jesus as my Savior at 13 or 14. I loved being saved and in a personal relationship with Jesus. I excelled in school and had a wonderful life.

The Turning Point

Then, at age 15 while I was at a football game, a guy who lived in my neighborhood asked me if I wanted a drink off a half pint of Yellowstone whiskey. I knew I should say no, but instead, I said, "I think I will." After drinking half the bottle, I loved the way it made me feel, so I drank more and more often until I barely graduated from high school.

I started wrecking cars and getting put in jail — stuff like that. I was in a serious car wreck at 18 that nearly killed me. My parents were told if they didn't rush to the hospital, they probably wouldn't see me alive again. Obviously, God had another plan, because I'm in my 70's now.

My alcoholism led to drug addiction too. I continued to

do lots of things I knew I shouldn't, and I became a slave to sin. At 25, I got an 18 year old girl pregnant and had a daughter. A couple of years later, she was pregnant again, and we decided to abort the baby. Then, nine years later, when we reconciled, we had another daughter.

Like me, she was also an alcohol and drug user. Sadly, when she stopped abruptly from using alcohol without any medical detox, she died from alcohol withdrawal at age 50.

A Revolving Door of Jobs

Regarding employment, after blowing my opportunities to go to college because my life was ruled by alcoholism, I got my first job in Frankfort, Kentucky, in 1968 at age 20. I promptly lost it because of my heavy drinking. I convinced my parents it was because I had run into and hung out with the wrong crowd, when really I was the wrong crowd!

So my dad set me up to work for IBM in Boca Raton, Florida. I got a cooler full of beer to drink on my way down there, and my alcoholic thinking kicked in. I thought it would be at least a year before I got a vacation, so I figured I should just go ahead and take one before I reported for work. I stopped in Daytona and drank up the rest of my money.

In desperation, I made a collect call to some guys I knew from Kentucky who were living in Orlando, and they came and got me. They were both drinking buddies, so I fit right in. One of them had a concrete company thriving due to Disney coming to town. I worked for him until I met a guy who dealt in Marijuana sales.

I started smoking weed, and I deluded myself into thinking this is the answer to my drinking problem. I thought I wouldn't drink as much when I smoked weed. That led to cocaine and drug addiction. I then started dealing drugs and did so from then until I got sober some 28 years later.

Returning Home

When I came back to Kentucky, I started doing painting jobs for my brother's company where he worked as an architect. While I was in Florida, I had started a painting business and did the same in Kentucky until I drank it away.

When my youngest daughter was born, I got a job at Circuit City and worked there until I was fired for having Marijuana in my car at work. (Interestingly, the guy who turned me in was deflecting attention from the fact he was stealing from the company at night!) I then bounced around at different types of jobs, quitting or getting fired because of my alcoholism.

Hitting Dead Bottom

Finally, I became virtually unemployable, and got a job as a car salesman. I was successful at that until I started drinking around the clock and couldn't report to work every day. That's where I was when I finally hit bottom. I decided that I just couldn't stand to live that way another minute. My life had become so futile, I began to wish I were dead.

So, after 34 years of alcoholism and drug addiction and slavery to every sin you can think of, I got on my knees and repented for all my debauchery and sin. I then cried out to God to please have mercy on my soul and please help me. He answered immediately!

As a first step, I was motivated to get medically detoxed in a behavioral hospital in Louisville. I was diagnosed as a chronic alcoholic by a psychiatrist.

Next, I got involved in an Alcoholic Anonymous 12 step program. It helped me a great deal with my alcohol and drug addiction. I soon became active in getting back to church, studying and applying scripture from God's Holy Word.

The real key to my spiritual renewal was listening on the radio every morning during my devotional time to Bob

Gary and Cathy Sims

Russell, who was the pastor of one of America's largest churches — Southeast Christian in Louisville, KY. Over a five year period, I figure that I listened to 1,300 of his sermons.

As for my parents, whom I put through hell, my dad died at 75 when I was 30 and still caught up in rebellion. But I was fully reconciled to my mom. In fact, I am convinced that my return to Jesus as a prodigal was due to the fact that she prayed for me every day of her life. She died at 92, and I had the blessing of speaking at her funeral.

Victory in Jesus

As a result, I have the peace that passes understanding in my life today. My prayer every day now is:

> Thank you Lord for saving my life, saving my soul and blessing me beyond all measure. Thank you for all you've done, all you're doing and all you're going to do. Thank you for all you've given me, all you've taken away and all that's left.

When I surrendered, I was living in abject squalor in an apartment by myself. Today I'm married to a godly woman, and we have two homes in Kentucky and a condo in Florida. Though I feel blessed to have what I have, these material things mean nothing to me compared to the grace and mercy shown me by God.

When I finally got to the point where I started believing that money, property and prestige meant nothing to me in comparison with my relationship to God, He blessed me to have an abundance of all of them. All praise and glory go to Him!

Conclusion

The story I identify with most in Scripture is that of the prodigal son (Luke 15:11-32). I was a prodigal for 34 years, and when I couldn't bear my life another minute, I came back to the Father begging for His mercy. He not only delivered mercy, but as the prodigal's father in the Bible did, He blessed me beyond all measure. His grace is more than sufficient, and I'm thankful for the abundant life He has given me and my wife.

People always speak of our Creator as "the God of a second chance." I don't buy that. I used up my second chance when I was 16. I have come to realize that He is a God of endless chances — full of grace, mercy and lovingkindness.

That's why I live with a heart full of praise.

"I never knew God was all I needed until God was all I had." — Gary Sims

"God seldom becomes a reality until He becomes a necessity." — Alcoholics Anonymous

Chapter 11

A Traumatized Child

"Come to Me, all who are weary
and heavy-laden, and I will give you rest."
(Matthew 11:28)

(Warren Hogan and his wife, Carol, live in Plano, Texas. He began his career as a metallurgical engineer. Today, he is a semi-retired business owner.)

Bang! Bang! Bang!

Oh, what happened? What just happened? It was November 1945. I was eight years old. I had been sleeping upstairs in the old farmhouse of my maternal grandparents.

The reason I was there was because two weeks earlier my mother had suddenly asked her brother to take her, my sister and me to her parents' house. Why? Because my father had stepped over the line. He was a heavy drinker and womanizer, and he was abusive to my mother. As such, he was a terrible role model for me and my sister.

The line he had crossed was his attempt to seduce my mother's younger sister!

A couple of weeks had gone by when my father unexpectedly showed up one night. A confrontation occurred in the kitchen between him and my mom. Also present were my grandmother and my uncle. My dad started to get a little out of control, and my grandmother told my mom, "Go, upstairs." She wanted to diffuse the situation before it got out of hand.

My mom started up the stairs when my dad pulled out a

38 pistol. He shot at her and hit her in the side. She spun around and fell to the bottom of the stairs. Then he fired the gun two more times, hitting both my grandmother and my uncle. It was the noise of these shots that woke me up. I had no idea what was going on.

So, I ran to the top of the stairs. I looked down and saw my mother laying at the bottom. As I started down the stairs, she began motioning at me to return to my room. That's when I noticed what appeared to be people on the floor who turned out to be my grandmother and uncle. At this point, my dad walked over to my mother and shot her again. But oddly enough, he shot her in the leg.

It was then that my 98 pound, five foot aunt from upstairs came running down the stairs yelling at my dad. She picked up a chair and started waving it at him, trying to shoo him out the door. He then turned around and ran out the door and into the nearby woods where he realized that he had really screwed up. And what do you think he did? He took the gun and shot himself!

So, when the smoke cleared, my grandmother and uncle were dead, and my mother was seriously wounded. Fortunately my mom survived, and she lived to be almost 95 — surviving the gun shots wounds, a heart attack and a stroke.

As for my father, unbelievably, he laid in the woods all night and didn't die. He crawled back up to the road where he was discovered and taken to the hospital. He spent the next 15 years in prison before being let out on parole, with the condition that he would make no contact with my family.

Coping with Tragedy

It was a very traumatic time, and our family was really screwed up. I can remember having frequent nightmares. Eventually I got back to school. I was nine years old and in the third grade. I was a very messed up kid.

One day, a little third grade girl looked me right in the eyes and said, “Why are you always moping around and asking for sympathy?” I guess I was. Can you image a third grade girl being that perceptive?

Well, that was unnerving. Over the next few days I started to process her question. And I had to acknowledge, my life was a mess. I wasn’t going any place. I didn’t want to be like my father! So, I decided at age nine, “I’m going to become somebody important!” I was not going to spend my life rotting away in jail.

So, how do you become a somebody special? I decided the only way was to excel in everything I tried to do. People would then say, “Isn’t he a great kid! Look at what he just accomplished.” Fortunately, I must have inherited that attitude from my mother. Her DNA was honesty and integrity, and it got built into my system. That’s what probably kept me out of jail.

Whenever I considered the God and Jesus stuff I kept hearing about, I asked, “What kind of a god would allow such a tragedy as this to occur in a child’s life?” So, I forgot about God and Jesus. I concluded that there was only one person in the world that I could depend on. Who do you think that was? It was me. Yes, I decided to depend on me and no one else. I’m going to excel. I’m going to be the greatest, and people are going to give me accolades.

Achievements

I did fantastic. I excelled in school. During my high school years, I played all the sports. I graduated in the top 10 out of over 400 students. My senior year I served as president of the National Honors Society, and co-captain of the football team. I was earning as many merit badges as possible. I was determined to prove to the world that I was somebody.

I went on to college where I did really well. I ended up

the number one student out of those who were majoring in metallurgical engineering. Everything was working well.

Meanwhile, in my private life, I had been dating a girl named Carol for several years, and in 1959 we decided to get married. Shortly thereafter, we started having children. Susan, our first child was born in 1960.

In the business world, I was a business gladiator, determined to fight my way to the top. I started out as a metallurgist working for Alcoa making aluminum castings. After four years, I changed my career direction and took a position at the bottom level of inside sales with Texas Instruments in Attleboro, Massachusetts. I excelled there, getting many promotions. After 20 years, I ended up managing a 1,000 man division with sales of $100 million per year.

I then had an extraordinary opportunity to come to Dallas, Texas, to serve as president and CEO of a $12 million electronic company with a goal of turning it into a $100 million company. In four years I was able to double the size of the company and position it to be recognized as the number one supplier in our industry segment.

Also during that time, I got involved in our trade association and quickly rose to become chairman of the Texas council. Now, "I was flying with the eagles." Talk about pride and ego — my ego was on steroids!

In 1987, I decided to start my own company. I called it "The Hogan Center for Performance Excellence." The focus was to help small and medium size companies to improve their business performance and achieve recognized world class distinction. We had a great run of 20 years, with ten of our clients being recognized as best companies in Texas and six of them going on to be recognized as best companies in America, receiving the Malcolm Baldrige Award.

I reveled in my success, thinking of myself as the model

of what a hard working, determined person could achieve. I had gone from the gutter to the penthouse, and I was very pleased with myself. All this while I considered myself to be a "righteous agnostic."

The Turning Point

Then, something happened that totally turned my life around. It was December of 2000. My wife and I had traveled to Seattle to celebrate Christmas with our oldest son, Christopher, and his family. As my wife and I were departing for home, our son handed me a little book titled, *More Than a Carpenter*, by Josh McDowell.

He told me that the author was a hardcore Atheist when he went to college and that his beliefs had been challenged by some Christians. He decided to start studying the Bible to see where their crazy beliefs came from. He was determined to prove them wrong. Well, guess what happened? He became convinced that he was wrong! So, he placed his faith in Jesus as his Savior, and he subsequently became a world renowned evangelist and defender of the Christian faith.

So, anyway, I didn't have anything better to do on my return flight. It was going to take me over three hours to get from Seattle to Dallas, so I decided to read what I considered to be a dumb, little stupid book. But before I got very far, I started running across some stuff I had never heard about, so my curiosity was aroused.

I was still a very left-brained engineering type. Give me some facts and figures, and I want to process them. So, the more I read of the evidence of creation presented in this book, the more my theory of evolution and Darwinism started to be challenged.

I spent a whole year talking to a lot of people, asking them why they became Christians. What was it all about? Finally, the week after the 9/11 attacks in 2001, I began to think that I was on the wrong team. This God and Jesus stuff was making a lot of sense to me.

It was at that point that I accepted Jesus as my Savior. But I was still thinking like an engineer. I began to wonder how I was going to explain my decision to others. And I started wrestling with the concept of Jesus as Lord of my life. How much of my life was I really willing to surrender to Jesus?

I had been the sole boss of my life since I was 9 years old. Am I really willing to give that up? Have I really become that crazy? I figured that if I died the next day, the odds were that I would go to Heaven — I didn't know for sure. But in any event, I thought I knew what I needed to do. As a new baby Christian, I had to start learning all about this Christian stuff. That's when the Lord provided me with a mentor for 24 weeks of one-on-one discipleship.

The Aftermath

While I was in the process of learning more about what it meant to live a Christian life, I was still a businessman. And just as I had taken the big step spiritually, the economy began to tank, particularly in telecommunications and semiconductors. On Friday, April 4, 2003, I suddenly perceived myself to be in a disastrous situation, and I didn't know how to fix it.

From the time I was nine years old I had always been able to find a solution to any problem. This time I just didn't know what to do! I was standing in the middle of my office when I faced up to this reality, and it was so jolting, I physically started to collapse. I couldn't think straight. I began to sweat profusely. My stomach turned upside down. I would have made a great advertisement for Prozac and Rolaids. I was really a mess!

A couple of days go by, and I'm at church with my wife and daughter. It happened to be communion Sunday. When I put the bread in my mouth, I finally surrendered my concerns to the Lord. And then, something miraculous happened. I had a tingling, radiant and euphoric experience. I went from the worst moment of my life to the best in a very short period of time.

Two hours later, I was in my car driving home when I started getting what I then called "brain waves." God began to reveal to me how I could resolve my problem. And then He added, "By the way, I've got greater things for you than just your business. Get prepared!"

The next couple of months were amazing. I was flooded with new contacts, and I was ready now to go to work in the Lord's kingdom! I suddenly realized that God couldn't use me before because I had not been willing to totally surrender my life to the guidance of His Holy Spirit.

Victories in Jesus

God began to work through me to accomplish things I never could have even imagined. Let me share just a few with you.

The first one was within my own church. It occurred around 2005 when a men's ministry was started that implemented what was called "The Top Gun Program." Within a few years, we had 90 men who had completed the program, learning the fundamentals of applied Christianity for their lives. I served in that ministry as a teacher and an organizer.

Next, I got involved in prison ministry. I've since participated in 27 different prison ministry events, and I've talked to hundreds of inmates. During that period of time, 62 of them have made professions of commitment to Christ. Now, I don't know about the long term, as that's between them and God whether it stuck or not. But I was out there planting a lot of seeds.

My next project is what I call my "Mac Ministry." I started using McDonald's like an office. I would go there to

Warren Hogan

get something to eat, and I would just sit there praying for God to give me an opportunity to witness Jesus to someone. Over the years I've met some very interesting people, and I've learned to be sensitive to their needs. Beyond witnessing Jesus to them, I have provided them food, given them a ride, prayed with them and helped them deal with their issues from a biblical perspective.

Another small ministry I've gotten involved in is called "Bezeugen," which in German means "to witness." It consists of distributing small Gospel tracts the size of business cards that can serve as great starters for a spiritual conversation.

Final Thoughts

Recently, I became curious about how many people in our nation are alive at 85, and how many are alive at 90 and above. I discovered that only about .7% of our 330 million people are males 85 and over, and only .2% are 90 and over. Wow! I processed that, and I concluded that at the age of 85,

I had only a 30% chance of making it to 90.

After having concluded that I am living on borrowed time, I decided that since my time left is very limited, I needed to make a plan for at least the next four years. So I made a list of things I want to accomplish. I divided them up among family things, business things and kingdom things And so, now at age 87, I've got a well-defined plan of what I am going to do.

Perhaps the most meaningful experience I have had since becoming a Christian is leading my mother at the age of 88 and my stepfather at age 90 to faith in Jesus.

Conclusion

If you are really a true believer, are you using your spiritual gifts to do the things that God wants you to do? Are you witnessing Jesus to the lost? Are you ministering to the poor? Are you standing for righteousness by speaking out about evils like sexual immorality and abortion?

One more thing, if you are feeling sorry for yourself and wallowing in self-pity, get over it! Get your eyes off yourself and onto Jesus. Lean on Him in faith, and then watch Him deal with your problems. Start counting your blessings. And your greatest is that Jesus died for your sins. Hallelujah!

To sum up my life, ***it has been quite a journey from tragedy to success to significance.***

Jerry Bridges

"Your worst days are never so bad that you are beyond the reach of God's grace. And your best days are never so good that you are beyond the need of Gods grace."

(Jerry Bridges, 1929 – 2016, in *The Discipline of Grace.* He was an evangelical Christian author, speaker and staff member of The Navigators, a Christian organization.)

Chapter 12

A Drug Addict

Hebrews 4

15) We do not have a high priest who cannot sympathize with our weaknesses, but One who has been tempted in all things like we are, yet without sin.

16) Therefore let us draw near with confidence to the throne of grace, so that we may receive mercy and find grace to help in time of need.

(Walter Colace is the pastor of a large church, called Christ Community Church, which is located in El Centro, California. The church operates a highly successful drug rehabilitation program.)

I was born into a loving family in El Centro, California in 1963. I was the second oldest of four boys in our family. My mother was from North Philadelphia and my father was an Italian from South Philly.

My father, along with two of his brothers, made the move from Philadelphia to the Imperial Valley in 1952 to work in the produce business. Mom and dad met at a dance in Yuma, Arizona, in 1960. Shortly afterward they were married. My father was 37 years old and my mother was 20. We were a close-knit family and prided ourselves on my father's Italian heritage.

In 1958 my father and one of his brothers started a small farming operation known as Colace Brothers. My father handled the growing and my uncle handled the sales in the office. They were growers and shippers of cantaloupes and lettuce with a reputation for quality. They worked hard to build a successful and respectable company. My father instilled in us a strong work ethic.

Growing up, my father raised us in the Catholic Church. We even attended Catholic school for a short period, and at one point, I was an altar boy. Even though I attended catechism, confirmation classes and received my first "Holy Communion" in the Catholic Church, I didn't know God or have a personal relationship with Jesus Christ.

The only reason we went to church was because our parents forced us to. My father would take us to confession every so often on a Saturday night and we would confess our sins to a priest who would then give us a penance which consisted of saying some "Hail Mary" and "Our Father" prayers.

My First Encounter With Hard Drugs

In my sophomore year in high school, I made a horrendous decision that would change the course of my life. I was drinking beer with some friends when one of them pulled out a bag of cocaine, a razor blade, a small round mirror and a glass straw. At that moment I became extremely nervous because I had never seen cocaine before and I knew I would be expected to participate.

As my friend chopped up the cocaine on the mirror with the razor blade, I could hear my father's voice from when I was younger, "Whatever you do, son, don't do drugs. They will destroy your life." Well, as the mirror was being passed around our little circle, each taking their turn to snort a line, my palms became clammy and I determined I wasn't going to do it.

But that changed suddenly when the mirror was passed to me. I caved to the peer pressure and snorted the cocaine. I was more concerned with what my friends thought about me than what my father said about drugs. The euphoric feeling I got from snorting the cocaine hooked me immediately and sent me on a 14 year run with drugs.

Spiraling Out of Control

Throughout my high school years cocaine became a part of my weekend party scene. But once I graduated from high school, my cocaine use became almost a daily routine. I even began freebasing the cocaine which is a chemical process that gives the cocaine a more intense high. Many times I would stay up all night drinking and smoking cocaine. My life was spiraling out of control.

In order to supply my cocaine habit I started dealing the drug. My addiction to cocaine was becoming more severe, and the more I sold, the more I used. I was losing touch with reality because of the large amounts I was using. The cocaine started creating a paranoia feeling within me and I started imagining that everyone was after me — law enforcement, friends and the people I had dealing for me.

I began to close the curtains in the small apartment I was living in and curl up in a corner of the bedroom, staring at the door for hours. I would wrap the cocaine in aluminum foil and stash it in places like the air conditioner vent and peanut butter jars in the refrigerator because I thought the DEA was going to raid me at any moment.

I even started carrying a Smith & Wesson .44 Magnum, what was called a "Dirty Harry Special." Life for me was becoming more delusional the more I used drugs.

Throwing Away My Career

When I was 22 years old my father opened another produce business called Sunrise Ranches. My father handled the growing and I was the main salesman in the office. My drug use not only continued but it escalated even more.

I started using cocaine almost every day and night. At times I would be up all night using the drug. My entire life was out of control. I was living in immorality and darkness. I couldn't control my drug habit, I couldn't control my personal life, I couldn't control my career. Sometimes I would go to the local bars and drink, getting into an occasional fight. I was even arrested a couple of times.

I ended up going through a couple of drug rehabilitation centers that were supposedly the best available in Southern California. They were 30 day secular programs that cost thousands of dollars, but they never got to the root of my problem, which was spiritual. Shortly after completing the programs, I found myself doing drugs again and even wondered if my bondage to drugs would take me to the grave.

Meeting My Wife

In 1986, I met the girl of my dreams. She had a very unique name — Grisel. I fell in love with Grisel at first sight. She had long brown hair, beautiful brown eyes and the face of an angel. Grisel was different from any of the girls I previously dated. When she smiled it captivated me, and there was a purity and innocence about her.

Before long, Grisel went to work at my office, and I got the opportunity to get to know her better. She was the daughter of a Pentecostal pastor, and she was a very sweet and caring person. The more I saw of her, the more convinced I became that I would marry her.

One day as I was on my way to work, I was involved in a serious auto accident. I suffered a bad pelvic injury and was confined to bed for a considerable time, experiencing traction and dealing with the pain with prescribed opiates.

During this season in my life, I hit a new low because I became addicted to the pain medication. I would use cocaine all day long and take pain pills during the night. It seemed like every ounce of life was being sucked out of me. I would call in sick to the office, and when I did show up, I was never in the right frame of mind.

Things got so bad that my father showed up at my apartment one day with legal papers for me to sign in order to remove my name from the business. My father said, "I love you, son, but I can't have you in business with me while you're on drugs." I denied the drug use to him while signing the papers on my glass coffee table that still had cocaine residue from the night before.

Looking For A Way Out

I figured the only way out of my bondage to drugs was to get clean and marry Grisel. When I proposed to her, she said yes, and I was overjoyed. However, I still had to get clean from the drugs and pain pills to which I was addicted. So, I entered a drug rehab program in El Cajon. It was a ranch operated by a couple who were former drug addicts themselves.

While in the rehab I met a man who was from New York. We were talking one day when he said, "Have you ever shot up heroine?" I said, "No, I would never put a needle in my arm." He replied, "Heroine gives you a high like nothing else ever could." He ended up convincing me to try it, and he somehow knew where to get it in El Cajon. He cooked the heroin in a spoon, drew it up in a syringe, found a vein in my arm, and shot it into me. I instantly loved the high it gave me, and I ended up doing it a couple of more times while in the rehab!

Grisel would visit me on occasion while I was in the rehab and we discussed our wedding plans. I didn't know it until later, but there were people, and rightfully so, who tried to stop Grisel from marrying me. They knew I was a drug addict and that it was wrong for her to marry an unbeliever. But the wedding plans moved forward.

On May 16th, 1987, Grisel and I married at the First Presbyterian Church in El Centro. The church was located on the same block as the former St. Mary's Church I was raised in. A parking lot was the only thing that separated the two churches. Grisel's father was an ordained minister with the Assembly of God denomination and officiated at the wedding. Even on our wedding day, I wasn't in my right mind. I had slept very little during the days leading up to the wedding, and I was drinking Scotch whiskey to take the edge off.

We honeymooned in Lake Tahoe for a week. After the honeymoon, we moved to Salinas, California for a new start. Prior to our wedding, I had been hired by a produce brokerage company as a salesman. I was excited to start over and thought my marriage to Grisel and the move to a new city would be the solution to my drug problem.

But my drug addiction wasn't a geographical problem — it was a spiritual one. It didn't take long for me to find a cocaine connection in Salinas. And to make matters worse,

Walter and Grisel Colace

the dealer I was scoring it from liked to shoot it through a syringe, and he turned me on to using it that way.

Heading for Destruction

Our marriage started heading for destruction because I was using cocaine after work and drinking in the bars at night. At times Grisel would find me in the bars and pull me out to go home. There were times when Grisel would talk me into going to church with her, but I kept rejecting God. This went on for a couple of years before I took a job with another produce company in Oakland, California.

My life was becoming very dark and depraved as I was using heroin daily. Things were becoming riskier because of the people I was doing drugs with. I couldn't believe the double life I was living. I was going to work early in the morning, slamming the heroin first thing when I arrived at the office, and then picking up more after work.

Grisel knew things were terribly wrong. My behavior was growing steadily worse. She saw bruising on my arm from the needles. When she asked me about it, I told her it was from moving produce crates.

One day she confronted me and said, "We need to talk." We decided that I would go on methadone to detox from the heroin. Methadone is a synthetic opioid, and it got me just as high as the heroin. Grisel would drive me to the methadone clinic in downtown Oakland to get my daily dose. The methadone didn't help me at all, and I started using heroin along with the methadone!

My behavior was becoming more erratic and destructive. I even started selling some of our possessions at a local pawn shop, including some of Grisel's things that had sentimental value. Our marriage finally reached the point where Grisel had done everything she could do to try and help me. There was no option left except to move out. She told me, "I'm not going to divorce you because I don't believe it's biblical, but I can't live under these conditions anymore."

After Grisel moved out, I started speedballing, which was mixing cocaine and heroin together in the syringe. I was losing all hope and the will to live. I didn't even care if I died. One evening I had done so many drugs that my heart felt like it was going to blow, and I started seeing things. To this day I believe I was seeing demons. I called an ambulance and was taken to the hospital. I remember staring up at the bright lights in the emergency room and thinking to myself, "What am I doing? I've thrown everything away. Why can't I stop using drugs?"

By this time I had lost my job and I was one step from being homeless. One night after I had done some speedballs, I found myself curled up in the place I was living, thinking I was going to die that night. I remember crying out, "God, if you're real, then save me!" A couple of days later Grisel stopped by and told me, "I know of a place you can get help. It's called Teen Challenge. If you will enter the program, then I promise you that I will work with you on restoring our marriage."

A New Creation in Christ

I flew to San Diego to get treatment at Teen Challenge. The staff member who welcomed me shared the Gospel with me and said that Jesus would forgive me of ALL of my sins and give me a new life. When he asked me if I wanted to repent of my sins and come to Christ in faith, I didn't even hesitate. I said, "Yes, I want Jesus." He led me in a prayer of faith, and I felt the weight of my sin lifted. Immediately, I fell in love with Jesus, and I knew He was going to make all things new.

In Teen Challenge I began learning the Word of God and how to pray. We were required to memorize scripture daily, and the classes were geared towards teaching us the Bible and how to live a Christian life. One of the first verses I memorized was 2 Corinthians 5:17, "Therefore, if anyone is in Christ, he is a new creation; the old has gone, the new has come!" This scripture in the Word of God went against everything I was taught in the secular drug rehabs. I was always taught, "once a drug addict, always a drug addict." But 2 Corinthians 5:17, which became my life verse, taught me that God gives us a new start in Christ and that the past is gone. We are new creations in Christ.

When I went through Teen Challenge they had a program called "Spiritual Emphasis" twice a year. It was a special time of ministry when they brought in guest preachers to minister to all the students in Southern California Teen Challenge for three whole days. It was amazing to worship with hundreds of men and women who were being delivered from a life of drugs, alcohol, gangs and prostitution. The Lord moved in powerful ways among all of us who were new in our faith.

I was only in the program a month when I attended my first "Spiritual Emphasis," and David Wilkerson, the founder of Teen Challenge, was one of our guest speakers. He preached a message and gave an altar call that changed my life. I committed to serving Jesus Christ for the rest of my life that night. I was already telling everyone about Jesus and even leading people to Christ. The joy and excitement I felt from knowing Christ grew stronger every day.

During my time at Teen Challenge God completely restored my marriage with Grisel. After graduating from the program, we moved in with my in-laws. We attended the church where they attended and where Grisel attended from the time she was a youth. I loved going to church with my wife, I was there every time the doors were opened. I was so grateful to the Lord for all He had done in saving me and giving me a new life.

I was hired by the church to reach out to others who were

in bondage to drugs and alcohol. I knew now that Jesus was the answer to the life-controlling problems people faced and I wanted to share the good news with everyone I could.

I started a Bible study that was open to anyone who had a drug or alcohol problem. Our first study had three people in it, but after 6 months we had to divide it into two separate nights with over a hundred people attending. The probation department even started sending us some of the people in their caseloads.

The Bible study grew into a residential program that was launched in April of 1994 and modeled after Teen Challenge. I called it "New Creations," and it was established as a non-profit organization with a governing board. It had residential programs for both men and women. In April of 2024 New Creations celebrated 30 years, and has impacted over 6,000 people.

A Church is Launched

In the summer of 1997, I was driving around El Centro when I saw the former St. Mary's Church I had attended when I was growing up. The church was now abandoned and everything around it looked dead. The grass was yellow, the palm tree leaves were overgrown and the walls were tagged with graffiti.

The Lord suddenly spoke to my heart to pull over. When I got out of the car, I looked down and saw a used syringe. I picked it up, and as I was looking at it, the Lord spoke to my heart and said, "There's going to be a church here." Immediately, I drove to the New Creations facility, rounded up the staff and told them what happened. We all climbed into one of the vans and went back to the church to lay hands on it and pray for it.

Following our time of prayer, I called a Christian businessman who owned property in the area to see if he could find out who owned the church. He called me a couple of weeks later and said, "I have the keys for the church for you, I'm going to lease it to you for a dollar a year."

During this time there were five couples, including Grisel and me, who were meeting at my cousin's house praying for the church. We were even praying for the right name. An aunt of mine suggested Christ Community Church. And on January 4, 1998, Christ Community Church held its first service. I couldn't believe that God had brought me full circle to launch a church in a building where I once confessed my sins to a priest and served as an altar boy!

When we launched Christ Community Church it grew quickly. Within the first six months there were over 350 people attending. We even bought the building from the Christian businessman for a fraction of what it was worth. He was very generous.

Directly across the parking lot stood the First Presbyterian Church, the one where Grisel and I had been married 13 years earlier. The congregation of that church had dwindled through the years, and they were meeting on Sundays in their fellowship hall. We met with the pastor to see if we could rent their main sanctuary on Sunday mornings. They agreed to lease it to us, and so we moved our Sunday morning services to their sanctuary in 2000. It didn't take long to fill their 550 seat sanctuary, so we ended up going to two services.

Because our church was growing so fast, the Presbyterian Church decided to sell their building to us for a price that was less than half of the appraised value. The ministry continued to grow as we reached out to the last, least, and lost of our community. We eventually had to go to three services, and we started looking for another possible location that would house more people. The Lord took care of this problem once again.

A Natural Disaster

On the afternoon of Easter Sunday in 2010, we experienced a 7.2 earthquake that struck the Imperial Valley. It shook the ground like nothing I ever felt before! At our house, dishes flew out of the cupboards and shattered on the kitchen floor.

I drove to the church immediately to see if there was any damage done to the building. Sure enough, the damage was obvious upon entering the church. Blocks of cement had fallen from the concrete beams of the 45 foot high ceilings. The walls were even split in some areas where you were able to see day light breaking through. That week the city engineer condemned the building.

We rented a local school auditorium to begin with. Then we were able to rent the Performing Arts Center until a new church could be built. We found ourselves in an unplanned building project, but God miraculously provided. From the time we tore our old building down, it only took a year and nine months to replace it. It was a miracle from the Lord!

Our new sanctuary has 1147 seats. Once again, God has miraculously provided! Further evidence of the miracle is that the one who built it is a former drug addict who graduated from New Creations in 1996 and started his own construction company in 2003.

Conclusion

God has blessed Christ Community Church through the years. We now have other campuses in other cities in the Imperial Valley, both English and Spanish congregations.

I could never take credit for any of these blessings. It was all the grace of God through our Lord, Jesus Christ. No words can fully describe His love, mercy, compassion and grace in my life, my family and my church.

I serve on the board of the Southern California Teen Challenge, which I consider an honor and a privilege, and I preach regularly at their Spiritual Emphasis events, where I first heard David Wilkerson give a message that changed the course of my life.

All praise and glory to God!

Grace Greater Than Our Sin

Julia H. Johnson (1849-1919)

(1910)

Marvelous grace of our loving Lord.
Grace that exceeds our sin and our guilt!
Yonder on Calvary's mount out-poured –
There where the blood of the Lamb was spilt.

Refrain:
Grace, grace, God's grace,
Grace that will pardon and cleanse within;
Grace, grace, God's grace,
Grace that is greater than all our sin!

Chapter 13

A Rock Musician

"Therefore if anyone is in Christ, he is a new
creation; the old things passed away;
behold, new things have come."
(2 Corinthians 5:17)

(Eric Barger has a dynamic ministry in Washington State called "Take A Stand! Ministries." He specializes in discerning apostasy in the church and defending the faith.)

My life was not unlike a lot of other kids growing up in the 1950s. I was the only offspring of my parents who themselves had no siblings. My father and mother met and married all too young and divorced before my recollection.

Due to my mother's advanced rheumatoid arthritis, which she had contacted at age 16, we lived with her parents. When my dad and mom split up, I was extremely fortunate that my grandfather and grandmother embraced and accepted the responsibility of raising me. I reflect back now and remember my grandfather as a man of honor and principle and my grandmother as the epitome of a loving mother. Though I didn't know my dad as I grew up, I am grateful that I was able to develop a rich and loving relationship with him before his passing in 2014.

Like most of you reading this, I was raised going to church. As a child, I attended a Methodist church in my hometown of Parkersburg, West Virginia. Every week I attended Sunday School. I took part in the usual activities such as church plays and camps and can still remember the various Vacation Bible Schools I attended. I was not a bad kid. I didn't cause a lot of trouble. I just fit into the crowd. If you had asked me if I were a Christian, I would have answered "Yes!" I heard all the great Bible stories, learned about the Bible's characters, and had some general understanding of the Christmas and Easter stories.

But to my remembrance, no one ever explained to me in a way that I understood that becoming a Christian was not a matter of engaging in a set of church activities or good works. Those things may be proof of one's salvation and relationship with God, but they are in no way the means by which to be saved.

Though I would have claimed to be a Christian and did all kinds of Christian things, like so many who have an unbiblical concept of Christianity, I did not possess the authentic salvation experience needed to cross the line between "lost" and "saved." I had never trusted Jesus as the Lord and Savior of my life. Instead, I had fallen into the pattern of just doing church stuff.

The Impact of Music

Early in my life, it became evident that I had musical talent. By age ten, I had begged my grandmother into buying me a guitar, and I began taking lessons. I learned the songs of the day, by ear, from the records I had purchased. My favorite musicians were The Dave Clark Five, The Supremes, Jan & Dean and The Beach Boys. Through listening to their records, I learned to play rock n' roll guitar.

In those days, the music being produced, and the lifestyle and attitude being advocated by the musicians, were vastly different from those of today. Then, the most rebellious song on the radio was Leslie Gore's "It's My Party And I'll Cry If I Want To!" It all seemed so harmless, but little did we know where the music revolution was going to take us. There were no songs glorifying drugs, the occult, murder, gangs, sexual acts or rape.

In the 1950s, record companies, the media and the public at large would have shunned any group or artist who glorified Satanism or suicide in their music. They would have found no audience. Yet today, themes like these garner for those who push them, all sorts of esteemed artistic awards and loving accolades from large fan bases. They also, of course, produce lots and lots of money.

I was first actually paid for playing music when a local disc jockey hired my band, "The Echoes," to play at an area teen dance. That was in early 1963, and I was only 11 years old! By the fall of 1964, our band was busy just about every weekend playing dances and parties.

Getting up to go to church on Sunday morning quickly became a thing of the past. After all, how could my grandparents expect me to do that since I had been out late the night before entertaining somewhere?

To put it frankly, since my grandparents had become less dedicated to church as I had grown older and since our home was at best a minimal witness for the Lord, I was allowed to slide and was not told that I had to attend church. Now don't miss this — you see, if Satan can separate a person from any sort of Christian fellowship, then he has accomplished a real coup in their lives.

Satan is continually working to undermine and destroy God's will and purpose for each and every life. As long as I was in church, there was always the possibility that I might have heard the Gospel presented in such a way that the Holy Spirit would have convicted me. I might have turned my life over to Jesus before the world, the flesh and the Devil could get a paralyzing hold on me.

But without any influence from Christians and only the fleeting memories of Sunday Schools from years gone by, Satan had me right where he wanted me, ensuring that I would fall for his plan for my life instead of discovering what

God wanted.

A Life-Changing Decision

A major part of Hell's plan for me began to unfold on a Sunday night in February 1964 when I first saw The Beatles. Watching their performance on the Ed Sullivan Show was a turning point for me, and probably thousands of other aspiring young musicians. I said, "That's what I want to do. I want to be a musician for life." Little did I know what that was going to mean for me.

By the time I turned 16, I was playing in the largest party bar at Ohio University six nights a week. I was popular and financially successful for my age. My high school English teacher even told me that I was making more money each week than she was!

I grew up too fast and I was growing up without godly guidance, having elected to follow the morals and lifestyle of my musical heroes. In short order, I had thrown off the upbringing that my grandparents had tried to give me, exchanging it for sexual experiences, drugs and the rock n' roll lifestyle. The idea of going to our little church seemed "weird," and "old fashioned" — in short, a waste of time. I gave it little or no thought as I soon had my eyes firmly planted upon myself and my selfish desires as the ultimate center of my universe.

It is certain that the biblical value system, which parents should employ, was sorely missing in our home. This is in no way a knock on my grandparent's character or upon their earnest desire to see me grow up right. However, one cannot teach what one does not know, and as I look back, it is apparent to me that instead of growing closer to God, our entire family moved farther away.

My grandmother had tried to deal with me, but I was out of control and not willing to listen much to what she or my grandfather had to say. I know I grieved them greatly in those days and only wish I had come to my senses in time to get things right with my grandfather before his death in the early 1970s.

A Degenerate Life Style

By hiding my sin — in particular my drug use — my grandparents knew relatively little of what was really going on in my life. It wasn't until years later that I allowed the truth to surface of how my teen years were spent with a joint in my mouth as I experimented with my newfound promiscuity. Life for me was the ultimate in "doing your own thing" — a prescription for certain disaster.

Some may wonder, "What's wrong with that? We live in a free society. Besides, everybody's doing it!" I understand that rationale. I felt that way for many years, living in my "do your own thing" existence. I couldn't see what harm could come from getting all of the self-gratification possible. After all, it was my life.

At 17, with one girl pregnant and my 23 year-old girlfriend very upset, I split for the West Coast. That was where it was all happening — success, possible stardom, fame and fortune. And for me, it would be a fresh start. But nothing in my life really changed except the scenery. By 21, I was playing regularly in Seattle area recording studios and nightclubs. Playing lead guitar and doing most of the arranging for the groups I was in, my songs were full of lyrics about love, but I didn't have a clue about what that word really meant.

Life had become one big "high." Sex, drugs and rock n' roll were all I really cared about. I was traveling with my band and living with a girl, while spreading myself around to any willing groupies. I was also taking mind expanding drugs like MDA, psychedelic mushrooms and LSD. These became my daily staples. All the while I was after the elusive record contract that would enable me to "make it" in the music business.

I started searching for reality in Eastern Mysticism — something we now call "New Age." I had a lingering affair with a bonafide practicing witch who dabbled in candle magic and astrology. I wanted to know why I existed and where I was going, but my very existence was distorted and the forecast for my future was at best "cloudy with limited visibility."

With my search for reality at a dead end, I found myself burnt out, disillusioned and in a fog. I left my band and invested what I had into a recording studio. It was there that I found the most success by worldly standards. From that first small studio, I moved through several others and finally became the studio manager for what is now advertised as one of the largest state-of-the-art recording complexes on the West Coast.

I had found my niche. I had a gift for hearing sounds and arranging music. Future Grammy Award winners Kenny G, the heavy metal group Queensryche and others were regulars there. I had my own production company, a Lincoln Continental, and more money than sense. I was on my way — to what, I didn't know, but I was going!

I continued to play in a local bar with friends "just for the party." That group was called "The Sin City Ramblers." With all of my apparent successes, I had actually hit the bottom, thinking I was heading for the top!

Another Turning Point

It was at this point in my life that I met a girl named Melanie. At first, she was destined to be no more than just another notch on my belt, another sexual trophy. But I really began to feel something different for her. After knowing her for only three weeks, I moved out of my girlfriend's house and did what I always said I'd never do — I got married!

Melanie and I had a lot in common. She had a library of

reference books on witchcraft and the occult. We were both into partying, drugs and rock n' roll. What else was there? In my confused mind, life was complete. But the bliss didn't last. It wasn't long before Melanie found that I couldn't be satisfied with just her. The scars of a life without morals were deep and impossible to change — or so I thought. Each day at home was a fight. Since I never knew what responsibility truly was, I ran to the things that made me feel good — my studio and my cocaine.

Marriage just didn't fit in my plans. Though we had eloped in what I thought was true love, the daily responsibilities of a committed life together hindered me. But, as far as I could understand what love was, I loved Melanie. What was I to do? I see now that I really loved the convenience of marriage, but had no understanding of the respect and care that comprises authentic unconditional love.

Seeking Help

We tried marriage counseling — the secular brand. After two visits, we both agreed that was a dead end. So on we went — drugging and drinking and partying and bickering. One night during a heated argument, Melanie threw a two-inch thick phone directory of yellow pages at me. I had made a smart comment about getting our lives straightened out through seeing another marriage counselor. Shaking off being nailed in the back of the head with the yellow pages, I picked them up, shook them at her, and for reasons unknown to me, I said, "But it's gotta be a Christian marriage counselor." She screamed, "You figure it out, you *@&$%!!" and slammed the bedroom door, locking it for the night.

The next morning I opened those same yellow pages to "religious counselors," closed my eyes and jabbed my finger at the page. I called the number my finger fell on, and a man answered, "Good morning and God bless you." The number I had called — at random, or so I thought — was that of a real live, Bible-believing, Christian minister who counseled people from the office of his real estate firm.

I explained that my wife and I had "problems," and we needed a counselor. In the back of my mind I kept thinking, "She is the one who needs help, so I'll get this counselor so she'll get off my back and leave me alone!" What I didn't realize was how desperately I needed help too, as well as our two daughters. After all, they had been raised in an ungodly environment where drugs ruled from behind closed doors and rock n' roll was the master of ceremonies.

During that first conversation with the counselor, he asked if we were Christians. I said, "Oh sure. We were both baptized in the Methodist church when we were babies." Besides, I was thinking, "What did he think we were? We weren't Hindu or something like that. We lived in America. Of course we're Christians!"

The counselor knew just by the way I had answered some of his questions that I didn't have any notion of who God was, and surely didn't have a personal relationship with His Son. To my knowledge, that was the first occasion in my adult life when I had communicated about anything the least bit theological with a born-again Christian. In all the nights I had performed in bars and concert halls, and on the many occasions I had traveled and conversed with people, I never recall anyone ever evangelistically sharing the salvation message of new life through Jesus Christ with me.

I had once even been hired to help write, record, and perform in a live presentation of a Christian "rock-opera" in which I played the part of the Apostle Peter no less! Yet, if anyone ever actually did challenge me about my need to know Jesus personally, it doesn't come to mind at all. What a tragic and telling indictment against the church in America!

Ted, the counselor, would eventually counsel Melanie and me separately or together over 50 times. It was during these sessions that he kept suggesting something that I didn't understand nor want — that I "take responsibility in our home." He also kept talking about the Bible — something I knew only as the "Good Book." In short, though I called myself a "Christian," I knew nothing about God.

After just two or three sessions with Ted, I began making up any excuse possible to get out of going to see him. However, Melanie kept going and was genuinely seeking and receiving help. She was immediately drawn to his presentation of Scripture. I however, felt very uncomfortable and wanted no part of this business. I know now that while she was being drawn by the Holy Spirit that God was also after me, but I wasn't at all willing or ready — yet.

I came home from the studio one evening in my usual state of being loaded on drugs to find a Bible sitting on the coffee table. I thought, "Well, isn't that nice . . . as long as Melanie doesn't get weird with it."

She got weird.

My Wife's Conversion

Melanie began to read the Bible, and supernaturally, God slowly drew her to faith in the Jesus that the pages revealed to her. She stopped being my drug partner. Our $500-$1,000 a week habit was now mine alone. Her speech changed. She stopped smoking, drinking and partying. She was different.

But my life was still on a downward spiral that came to a head when she cajoled me into going to another counseling session. When Ted asked in closing, as he always did, if either of us wanted to "receive Jesus as Savior," Melanie said yes. With huge tears flowing down her cheeks, he led her line-by-line in a prayer of commitment. I watched as my wife made an open confession of her faith. But I determined that no way was He getting me!

I felt like Melanie had "flipped out" and become a "Jesus

freak." I'd had it. I promptly packed a bag and left her for several days, but as time passed, I missed her and our girls and I was getting tired of sleeping on the floor at the recording studio. So, back I went to find that her witchcraft books were gone — not because a well-meaning Christian had advised her to throw them out, but because God had already dealt with her heart that she only needed ONE book.

She had also discovered "Christian" music, and I had to admit that it was indeed pretty good. It had life and was a far cry from what I had always thought of as church music. My concept of Christian music was an organ playing in a minor key that made you depressed and want to cry.

There was one more change. Over the span of just a few days, Melanie had become like the Apostle Paul's sister! But when she realized that preaching at me was not going to facilitate any change, she started loving me unconditionally, which was nearly unbearable. It was then that I began to feel an inkling of what I now understand to be the drawing of the Holy Spirit as He began wooing my heart through my wife.

Still, I rejected God. Though He was showing me close up in Melanie what He can do to cleanse and restore a life, I was deeply entrenched in my hopeless condition.

Weeks passed, then months. We were still together, in theory, but it was anything but happy or peaceful. Melanie read her Bible and attended a Bible study group and church services, while I plunged deeper into cocaine and my work. She was going to Heaven, while I was going to Hollywood! I had lost my drug buddy and partner in perversion but I was still determined to follow "my dream," regardless of what it cost or where it led.

My Conversion

Then, one Friday night Melanie discovered my car close to a girlfriend's house. Though she didn't catch me there, I knew I'd been caught by the note she left on my windshield.

That night I did as much coke as I ever had, throwing me into a state of hyper-paranoia. I spent the next day in a hotel room trying to "come down." The coke had taken me into a new level of experience but not a good one. I couldn't stop shaking, and my worst fear was realized when I found my dealer had run out of the white powder I craved.

Melanie spent that day praying and crying to God for direction. She and our counselor had prayed together on the phone at one in the morning: "God . . . whatever it takes . . . GET ERIC!"

Sunday was a cold, rainy Seattle day. Melanie went to the bookstore to find something that would give her peace. Finding nothing on "peace," she walked out with *Racing Toward Judgment* by prophetic author David Wilkerson. Reading it entirely, her mind had been diverted from dwelling on me. For all she knew, I could have been dead by then, but she was comforted with the peace that only knowing God can give.

My memory blurs on the actual chronology of events from those days. Concerning what happened that night, Melanie has had to help me accurately reconstruct this story. She says that in my drunken state, I came through our front door screaming obscenities at her. Just as had been my habit, I began blaming her for all our problems. This is often the kind of demented psychology that individuals execute on others, when they are themselves unwilling to take responsibility for their own failings.

At some point, I simply sat down on the floor and passed out. Two hours later, I came to with perhaps the worst drug and alcohol hangover of my life. I hadn't slept in three days. I had overdosed severely, and had been drinking heavily for most of that period. All I had on my mind was finally ending our ruined marriage — the reason I had come back to our house earlier that night.

I climbed up onto the couch where she had been sitting quietly praying for me. Confused and depressed, I was trying to muster up some sort of cowardly courage to inform her that after throwing the word "divorce" at each other in our fights month after month that I was finally going to do it. It was at that point that I picked up the book that was lying there between us. In my nervousness, I simply flipped *Racing Toward Judgment* open to page 60. There on the left side of the page, underlined with my wife's pen from just hours before were three words: "GOD HATES DIVORCE!"

It was then — at the lowest state of my life — that I finally reached out to God.

I fell on the floor and burst into tears. My wife began to cradle me in her arms. I know now that through her, Jesus was hugging an adulterous, abusive, drug addict. I genuinely pleaded with God (and my wife) to forgive me. I'd said I was sorry to her before, but only because I had been caught. This time however, I had hit the bottom and I really meant it. I was finally crying out to the God who I had heard about in that Methodist Sunday School two decades earlier, and who had radically transformed my wife, delivering her from the same pit that He was now pulling me from.

I was forgiven right then and there of every evil thing I had ever done. How am I sure? Because the Bible promises that "...whosoever calls on the name of the Lord SHALL BE SAVED" (Joel 2:32 & Romans 10:13). You might ask, "But how can you trust the Bible?" One of the simple truths that separate the Bible and Christianity from every other religion is the historical fact that Jesus Christ died and rose from the grave. I had searched enough for "inner enlightenment" to know that the answer to life didn't lie inside of me or in the teaching of dead sages.

For the first time, I had an inexpressible feeling of whole-

Eric and Melanie Barger

ness and value. I was clean. I was saved! And although I never checked into a drug or alcohol rehabilitation center, I miraculously never experienced any withdrawals from the years of substance abuse. God's Holy Spirit came and did it all!

But What About You?

My prayer is that you won't have to "hit the bottom" on your way to what you think is the top. You don't have to. How tragic it is that so many people, like me, have to get to their very lowest place before they look around and realize the mess they are in and come to an understanding that they can't solve it alone.

Though many people comment to me that we have a "great" testimony, I really wish my story were much different. I wouldn't wish what Melanie and I experienced all those years on anyone. More than once I have wrapped my arms around my now-grown daughters and asked their forgiveness for the things I did during their formative years, most of all for just neglecting to be a good, loving dad.

Some "church people" hear a story like ours and think, "My, they really needed God. Isn't it nice that they got straightened out?" But you need to understand that each and every person needs the same cleansing experience from life's sins that Melanie and I received.

As human beings, we share in common the fact that we have each sinned (Romans 3:23). Yet many want to rationalize that they are surely better than most and believe that God must grade on a curve, sending only the really bad people to Hell.

But as much as some want to believe so, that is not what the Bible teaches. God does not judge on the curve. It is a lie of Satan and part of our flawed human thinking to believe that God will accept us just because we're good and kind or that any good works we could accomplish can save us eternally.

The fact is there is nothing — no good deeds or human works — that we can ever do that can save us (Ephesians 2:8-9). To believe that we can redeem and then save ourselves is a deception that will take millions of people on a one-way trip to Hell (Romans 6:23). But you don't have to go there, and God has provided a way out!

God's Grace

Because of God's great love for us, Jesus Christ came to earth and sacrificed Himself for us. He took our place and paid the penalty for each and every one of our sins. He died and was resurrected, and in doing so, He triumphed over death, Hell and the grave.

He has already paid the price for you to enter God's Heaven — forever. All you have to do is first ask Him for forgiveness, and then decide to repent, that is, turn from your sins and follow Him with all your heart.

He didn't come to spoil your fun or ruin your life. Jesus came to provide us with abundant life (John 10:10). He offers real, lasting peace and joy for our lives on earth and for all eternity! The joy and peace of knowing Him is the greatest high I've ever known. This is NOT "religion." This is a personal relationship with the Creator of the Universe!

Tim Keller

"We certainly should be very active seeking God. Jesus Himself called us to 'ask, seek, knock' in order to find Him. Yet, those who enter a relationship with God inevitably look back and recognize that God's grace had sought them out, breaking them open to new realities."

(Tim Keller [1950-2023] was the founding pastor of Redeemer Presbyterian Church in New York City.)

Chapter 14

A Scam Artist

"People with integrity walk safely, but those who follow crooked paths will be exposed."
(Proverbs 10:9)

(Robert Russell was delivered from being a con artist to being a street minister for Jesus. He and his wife, Blanca, live in Dallas, Texas, where they conduct a ministry to the homeless.)

I was born out of wedlock in Galveston, Texas, in 1943. My mother married when I was two years old, and my stepfather adopted me, giving me his last name of Russell.

My dad never gave me any problems because he basically ignored me. The only advice I ever remember him giving me was, "Don't do the crime unless you are willing to do the time." My dad managed to stay employed at a minimum income job even though he was an alcoholic.

My mom was a very troubled person. She was probably what would be diagnosed today as bipolar. She could be as sweet as an angel one moment, and then a moment later she would be screaming and cursing like mad. When I was around her, I was very cautious, like I was walking on eggs, because I never knew what would suddenly set her off!

My mom and dad argued constantly. Much of this was probably due to the fact that both of them cheated on each other. As a family, we were what was called in those days, "poor white trash." I suffered from very low self-esteem. I always felt like an ugly duckling.

The only person I admired as a teenager was a cousin of mine who was four years older than me. He paid attention to me, and I admired the fact that he was a gangster! He did one of the first drive-by shootings I ever heard about. Looking back on it now, I'm thankful that he never tried to recruit me to join his life of crime.

Coming of Age

In 1960, when I was 18, I basically ran away from home and joined the Marines. I just couldn't take all the chaos at home anymore.

I tested out in the Marines as an expert marksman. Because of this, the decision was made to assign me to the military police! I thought they were nuts. I had spent my teen years running from the cops, and now I was one! And, to say the least, I was not a good one.

I was always in trouble with my commanding officer because I followed in my dad's footsteps by becoming a heavy drinker. Thus, I was always getting into trouble for getting drunk and carousing. I often had to spend some time in the brig on "champagne and cake," which was my term for "bread and water."

When I was released from the Marines, I decided to use my military police experience to seek a law enforcement job in California, but I was told I was too short. (I'm 5' 5" tall.) So, I went to work for a company that manufactured fuel injectors. That didn't last long before I decided to return to Houston.

My First Marriage

I got a job working in a steel mill, and I met the sweetest girl I had ever encountered. I fell head over heels in love with her, and we got married. But I was continuing to drink, and I developed a new vice. I became a serial adulterer.

My wife began to exhibit increasing signs of mental instability. One very hot night she caused a major disturbance in our neighborhood, and she was arrested. Tragically, the police put her in a paddy wagon and forgot about her, and she died of a heat stroke!

New Employment Adventures

When the steel mill closed, I decided to try my luck with the real estate business which had always intrigued me. I got a license and started selling homes. I proved to be good at it — so good, in fact, that before long, I was made the president of the small real estate company that I worked for.

At that point, I shifted the company to commercial real estate and started advertising in the *Wall Street Journal* in search of investors. I was contacted by some New York high rollers who were interested in the properties I had found.

These guys called me to arrange a visit to Houston. They must have had me on a speaker phone because I could hear several of them laughing at me in the background. They started referring to me as a "hillbilly," and that riled me.

So, when they arrived in their expensive suits carrying their fancy leather brief cases, I met them wearing jeans and a tie-dyed t-shirt. But I was also driving a Rolls Royce, which caused their eyes to bug out. (Actually, the Rolls Royce belonged to a friend.) Anyway, they started treating me with respect.

After completing a few lucrative deals with this group, I decided to resign from the real estate company I was working for and form a company of my own. I would find major properties — usually large apartment complexes — and I would purchase these with funds I had raised from investors. I would then renovate and convert them into condos and sell them at a substantial profit.

For example, I made $750,000 over a three year period — and that was 50 years ago when that amount was equivalent to $4 million in today's purchasing power. I ran through this money at the speed of light while drugging, drinking, partying and compulsive spending on "stuff." For example, I had a Lincoln Continental Mark 4 that was silver on the outside and red inside. All I needed was a big hat and a couple of girls, and I would have been in business as a pimp!

Yes, I was making a lot of money and living high. There were times when I had so much money that I would take a year off and just enjoy life. To me, being on top of the world consisted of being laid back in a comfortable recliner while eating a Hershey bar, smoking a weed and listening to Elton John sing. Yet, I had a nagging emptiness inside that I could not satisfy.

I decided to buy half interest in a home building company, which proved to be a big mistake. I quickly went broke, but when you are a high roller like I was, that is no big deal. Going broke was part of the business.

I looked around for another fast money opportunity and found it with a guy in New York who was in the oil business. I joined him in selling drilling shares on leases we had bought. This business was a complete sham from the beginning. We were selling shares of what we knew would be dry holes. And we were violating the law in two ways — first, by selling unregistered securities, and second, by selling them without a license.

We made a lot of money, and when I look back on that venture today, I realize that it was only the grace of God that kept me out of prison. Throughout this venture I constantly feared the FBI would knock on my door any day, but it never happened.

A Second Marriage

In 1983, while working in the Dallas area, I met a hot Mexican lady who was a real knockout, and I fell for her. We quickly decided to start living together in one of the condos

I owned. Her name was Blanca, and one day, out of the clear blue sky, she suddenly said, "I want to go to church." I was astounded. I hadn't been to church in years, and I had no interest in visiting one. But she was insistent.

As we began arguing about her idea, I discovered that she had even picked out the church she wanted to visit. It was a small Baptist church that appeared to be experiencing hard times.

I started arguing that if we were going to visit a church, we could at least find a very nice one with big stain glass windows. But she insisted on the small church. So, very reluctantly, I went with her, expecting the worse.

To my surprise, the people were very friendly and receptive of us. They didn't look down their noses at us. We felt loved. The preacher was so young that he looked like he was right out of high school, but I was fascinated by his down-to-earth, life-relevant sermons.

The Great Turning Point

Before long, we were going to the church every Sunday morning and evening and also on Wednesday nights. It didn't take long for me to realize that the reason Blanca had suddenly gotten interested in church was because she wanted to get married. She figured that if we started attending church, it would lead to marriage, and it did in 1983.

It also resulted in my salvation the same year. That started my sanctification, which was going to take considerable time since I knew nothing about the Bible. For example, one day I was sitting in the tub reading the Bible when I cried out to my wife, "Hey, honey, you won't believe what I just read in this book. It says that it is more blessed to give than to receive! Isn't that the craziest thing you've ever heard? Which would you prefer — to give a Corvette or to receive one?"

Blanca and Robert Russell

But the Lord was working on me, slowly smoothing off my rough edges as I learned more and more about how a Christian should live.

A major turning point for me occurred while reading the book of James. I came across James 1:27 which reads: "Pure and undefiled religion before our God and Father is this: to visit orphans and widows in their affliction, and to keep oneself unstained by the world."

That verse penetrated my heart and motivated me to seriously respond to it. So, I proposed that we sell everything we owned, move to Mexico and start feeding and clothing widows and orphans. At first, my wife was resistant. She was not excited about moving to Mexico. But I strongly felt God's call to go there, and she finally agreed.

Missions Work

In 1983, we gave up all our material goods and moved to

a city in Mexico called Taxco, located about 100 miles southwest of Mexico City. I knew that once we ran through our funds, I would need to support ourselves and our ministry in some way, and Taxco was famous for producing some of the finest handmade silver jewelry in the world.

I figured I could make trips back to the States from time to time to sell the jewelry and then return to Mexico with American items that Mexicans would be interested in buying. That idea worked out well, and I was able to produce enough funds to feed and clothe the poor people of that area — and use that opportunity to share the Gospel with them.

One of my most interesting experiences in Mexico was based on a relationship I developed with an American I met in Acapulco. He was a graduate of the University of Texas and came from a wealthy family. He had used some of his wealth to purchase a night club in Acapulco.

I began witnessing to him, and he seemed to come under conviction. He started agreeing that he needed to get out of his worldly business and get his life together, but he never took action to do so.

I eventually lost contact with him. Years later, after we had returned to the States, he contacted me to let me know that not only had he accepted the Lord but he was now the pastor of a church of one thousand!

My wife and I ran our ministry in Taxco for 20 years until it became too dangerous for Americans to live in that area due to increasing crime. But before we left, we were greatly blessed when a young woman we had been helping decided to give us her baby boy whom she felt she could not support. We adopted him and raised him in the Lord. We are now grandparents through him and his wife.

Ministering to the Homeless

When we returned to the States, I had no idea what kind

of ministry the Lord wanted me to get involved with. But it didn't take long for my heart for the poor to clarify what direction I should take.

One day my wife and I went to a donut shop, and as we were entering, I noticed a black man leaning against a car out front. He looked desperate, so I asked if I could buy him some donuts and milk, and he agreed.

A couple days later, I'm driving around in the same area, and I see him walking down the street looking very ragged. I stopped and bought him some chicken. It was after those two encounters with him that I started noticing many others like him who were living on the streets, and I decided to start ministering to them daily.

So, I started cooking beans and other items to give out to the homeless and hungry. As I fed them, I made it a point to assure them that they were loved by Jesus and that He was willing to forgive them of their sins and give them a new lease on life.

Conclusion

The ministry began to grow, and today we are supplying hundreds of meals per month as well as other services to the homeless. I named the ministry, "The Flashlight Street Ministry," because we are devoted to shining the light of Jesus into the very dark world of the homeless.

God has given me a supernatural love for these outcasts of society. I'm dealing daily with gangsters, pimps, prostitutes and drag queens. I want them to know that Jesus loves them and that He is willing to forgive them and save their souls, just as in His amazing grace He has forgiven me and redeemed my life.

Praise the Lord!

Chapter 15

A Homosexual

1 Corinthians 6

> 9) Do you not know that the unrighteous will not inherit the kingdom of God? Do not be deceived; neither the sexually immoral, nor idolaters, nor adulterers, nor effeminate, nor homosexuals,
>
> 10) nor thieves, nor the greedy, nor drunkards, nor revilers, nor swindlers, will inherit the kingdom of God.
>
> 11) And such were some of you; but you were washed, but you were sanctified, but you were justified in the name of the Lord Jesus Christ and in the Spirit of our God.

(This a remembrance of a dear friend, written by the author of this book.)

In 1980, the Israeli Knesset (the nation's Parliament) passed a law recognizing Jerusalem as the undivided, eternal capital of the nation of Israel.

There were three immediate responses to this legislation — two negative and one positive. The Arab nations united to institute an oil embargo against European nations and the United States, resulting in skyrocketing gasoline prices and long lines at the gas stations. A second response took the form of 13 national embassies in Jerusalem closing and moving to Tel Aviv. The third response, the positive one, was a decision on the part of Christian friends of Israel to establish an International Christian Embassy in Jerusalem as an effort to encourage the Jewish people and their government.

As a part of the founding of the Christian Embassy in September 1980, a celebration of the Feast of Tabernacles was held in Jerusalem. It was attended by approximately 1,000 Christians who came from all over the world.

The reason for selecting that particular feast to celebrate was based on a prophecy in Zechariah where he says that during the future millennial reign of Jesus over all the earth, each nation will be required to send representatives to Jerusalem each year to celebrate the Feast of Tabernacles. And, in fact, Zechariah said that any nation that fails to do so will have rain withheld from it (Zechariah 14:16-17).

Over the years since that time, this annual week long celebration in Jerusalem has grown to an attendance of over 3,000 from 80 different nations.

Experiencing the Celebration

It was my blessing to take a group of 50 Christian pilgrims to this celebration in the Fall of 1987. I had no idea what we were going to experience. That was before access to the Internet, so there was very little I could find out before we attended.

To say the least, I was astounded! It turned out to be the most spiritually refreshing and enriching experience of my life. There were people present from all over the world. Most of the sessions were held in the largest auditorium in Israel. One session was held outdoors in the desert at the site of Qumran on the Dead Sea.

Later in the week, the celebration ended with all the participants gathering at the top of the Mount of Olives for a songfest. Then, we marched down the mount and around the Old City of Jerusalem, carrying banners that expressed our support of Israel.

But most important of all, we were introduced to Davidic Praise Worship. This is a type of worship that utilizes the visual arts, singing and movement. We saw skilled dancers moving beautifully while waving colorful banners to the thrilling Jewish rhythms.

The Spiritual Significance

And it was not just performance. It was much more than that. It was worship services of total immersion of the senses, during which the worshipers were drawn into participation by singing, waving their hands and banners, clapping, shouting and dancing in the aisles. I personally had never experienced anything like it, and I was deeply stirred in my spirit. I felt like I was witnessing Psalm 150 before my very eyes:

> 1) Praise Yah!
> Praise God in His sanctuary;
> Praise Him in His mighty expanse.
>
> 2) Praise Him for His mighty deeds;
> Praise Him according to the abundance of His greatness.
>
> 3) Praise Him with trumpet blast;
> Praise Him with harp and lyre.
>
> 4) Praise Him with tambourine and dancing;
> Praise Him with stringed instruments and pipe.
>
> 5) Praise Him with resounding cymbals;
> Praise Him with clashing cymbals.
>
> 6) Let everything that has breath praise Yah.
> Praise Yah!

I realized that what I was experiencing was a fulfillment of Bible prophecy that says the Tabernacle of David will be resurrected in the end times before the return of the Messiah (Amos 9:11-12).

The Tabernacle of David was very different from the Tabernacle that Moses built in the wilderness. Moses' Tabernacle was a worship center of animal sacrifice. It was very ritualistic in nature. In sharp contrast, David's Tabernacle consisted of a single, simple tent that contained the Ark of the Covenant. Whereas the High Priest entered the Holy of Holies in the Tabernacle of Moses once a year to offer a sacrifice for the sins of the nation, the Tabernacle of David was open to worship before the Ark 24 hours a day, and priests constantly danced, sang and shouted praises in joyous celebration (1 Chronicles 16:6 & 37).[1]

The form of worship David introduced was so radically different that he felt obligated to justify it by pointing out that it had been ordained by God through two prophets — Nathan and Gad (2 Chronicles 29:25).

The Tabernacle of David served as a bridge between what had become the ritualistic, lifeless worship of the Tabernacle of Moses and the more splendid form of worship that would characterize the Temple of Solomon. And in like manner, the revival of Davidic Praise Worship today is serving as a bridge from the Church Age to the Millennial Age. It is also providing the joyous, celebratory atmosphere for the welcoming of the Lord's soon return.

The Relevance to This Book

The key figure in the revival of Davidic Praise Worship in our day and time has been a man named Randall Bane. He was born in Albion, NY, in 1941 and died in Medina, NY, in 2021 at the age of 80. The two small towns are located only 10 miles apart just south of Lake Ontario in upstate New York.

I never learned much about Randall's early life. All I know for sure is that he once told me he was "a church-going kid" who never responded to the Lord. After high school, he joined the Army and served during the Vietnam era. He attended college briefly, but quickly dropped out and headed for New York City to become an actor.

The art world of New York was not a good atmosphere for Randall for by the time he arrived there, he had become a practicing homosexual. The only thing he ever told me about his life there was that "it was morally depraved." He said that after almost a decade of acting, while supplementing his income driving a taxi, he looked in the mirror one morning and said to himself, "If I keep this lifestyle, I will be dead of AIDs in five years."

So, in 1974, at the age of 33, he decided to flee New York into the loving and forgiving arms of Jesus. He became a Christian and decided to devote the rest of his life to using his talents and spiritual gifts to serve the Lord.

His New Career

Randall Bane as Obie Good.[2]

The first thing Randall did was to develop a mime character called, "Obie Good, the Love Clown." Simultaneously, he started presenting visual interpretations of Christian songs. He took his portrayals to churches, conferences, festivals and television.

In 1984, at age of 43, Randall was invited to form a team of dancers to exhibit Davidic Worship at the Christian celebration of the Feast of Tabernacles in Jerusalem. He selected Valerie Henry to serve as choreographer. He had met her at a CBN Summer Music Seminar in Virginia Beach, Virginia.

The two of them combined their formidable talents to revolutionize the Feast celebration, and they continued to work together annually at the Feast for the next 12 years.

Valerie Henry wrote these words about Randall after he died:[3]

> In our ministry together, I witnessed Randall's amazing creativity, how he affirmed others in their gifts and talents, and how he could consistently draw out the very best in others. He was a master at blending various levels of movement proficiency, and often converged dance with gestures and dramatic expression.

While working together, Randall and Valerie took the Feast Dance Company on tours to nations all over the world. They also introduced an international audience to Davidic Praise Worship through the videos of the annual Feast celebration which participants took back home with them.

Reflections on Randall's Ministry

Most people always considered Randall to be primarily a dancer. He was not. He had never had any dance training when he went to New York City to become an actor. Further, at age 33, he considered it too late in life to start dance lessons. But he soon discovered that he had a natural gift for fluid movement, and so he decided to develop that gift by "sweating into it" through constant practice.

In 1996, Randall opened what he called "David's House" in Kansas City, Missouri. He made this house the base for his ministry to teach people the nature and importance of Davidic Praise Worship.

One aspect of Randall's ministry that particularly ap-

Dr. Reagan with Randall Bane

pealed to me was his solo interpretations of the Bible story songs recorded by Ken Medema. In these he beautifully combined his talents for both acting and movement.

In the early 1990s, after I had been introduced to Randall and his worship revolution at the 1987 Feast celebration in Jerusalem, the ministry I headed up decided to hold a worship conference in Houston, Texas. Randall was invited to conduct the conference.

I had been flying to Houston once a month for a long time to speak at a church there on Sunday morning. Our worship conference was scheduled for the Saturday before that Sunday I was supposed to speak at that church. I called the elders of the church and suggested that they replace me with Randall. They refused.

However, some of them came to the conference, and when they saw Randall's brilliant and anointed interpretation of Ken Medema's song about Paul and Ananias, they came to me and said, "We don't want to hurt your feelings, but we have decided that we would like to have Randall instead of you tomorrow morning!"

So, Randall stayed over, ministered to the church, and was invited back many times. That's how exciting he was!

Conclusion

I will be forever grateful to the Lord for bringing Randall into my life. Even more, I am grateful for how Jesus saved his life and radically changed it — delivering Randall from decadence to righteousness.

Chapter 16

A 1960s Rebel

"... the rebellious dwell in a parched land."
(Psalm 68:6)

(Evelyn Hinds and her husband, Robert, live in the mid-cities area between Dallas and Ft. Worth, Texas. Both are very active members of their church where Evelyn serves as a women's Bible teacher.)

I was born in September of 1949 in Clinton, Arkansas. I was the second of seven children. I was a quiet kid and remained that way during my teens — mainly because my dad was a very volatile person. I coped with his temper by staying quiet and out of his way.

My mother had five children coming of age in the 1960s, and the worst of her problems was my father. He divorced my mom in 1975, but he told her he wanted to keep in communication with his children. The problem was that none of us wanted to talk to him. He couldn't understand that. He was so focused on himself, he had really no interest in others. It was a very sad situation. My dad lived to be 80, but his final years were clouded with dementia.

In contrast, my mother was over-the-top good and loving. She did all she could to help the rest of us cope with the hardships caused by my dad.

Off to College

My family moved to Kansas City, Missouri, soon after I was born. My dad began work as an air traffic controller there as I grew up. We occasionally attended a Methodist church, but there was no emphasis on having a personal relationship with Jesus.

When I graduated from high school in 1967, I headed to Lawrence, Kansas, to attend the University of Kansas. I arrived on campus with a small trunk with what I thought were appropriate college clothes. It wasn't long until I realized I only needed a couple of pairs of jeans and some tee shirts.

Bob Dylan was my hero and he sang, "The Times They Are A Changing." Indeed they were, but not in the good way that I had hoped. College campuses were hot beds of radicalism. Students were caught up in rebellion against "the establishment." Hard drugs and free sex were the craze.

I had made a decision to go my own way. I was a very independent young woman, but I was definitely allowing the times to influence me. I never called myself a hippie but others would have. I was a person caught up in rebellion.

I quickly dropped out of the University of Kansas, and scrapped my plans to pursue teaching. Dropping out was not unusual back then. I was a 19 year-old "child of the 60s," and dropping out was in the air. I decided to marry my boyfriend, so I packed two suitcases and set out for a new life.

Fleeing to New York

It was Christmas day in 1968 when I left my family in Kansas City, and boarded an airplane bound for New York City. Lyrics from Peter, Paul, and Mary's current hit song, "Leaving on a Jet Plane," played in my head. I could really identify with the phrase that said, "Don't know when I'll be back again."

My boyfriend was a born-and-bred New Yorker. He was older than me and seemed to have life figured out. I thought I did, but I hit a snag in the form of a health problem that sent me into a deep, dark depression.

Marriage seemed like the only decision I could make. My boyfriend proposed, and I decided to go ahead and give it a try. I was also trying to get as far away as I could from my Midwest upbringing. I set out to begin a new life in an apartment in the Queens section of New York City. I hoped to become a different and happier person.

Broken Dreams

I expected to live in New York for the rest of my life. I had no reason to believe that my husband would ever consider moving out of "The Big Apple." However, I suffered from loneliness and depression in the big city.

My happiest moment came with the birth of my son, John Wesley, in 1973. However, more suffering came when we learned that he had a very serious medical problem.[1] When his problem was revealed, I cried out to God, "How could You let this happen? Is this Your punishment for me?" I sank into a deeper depression.

It was no surprise that my marriage didn't work out, given the fact that I knew very little about God, and I was self-centered. I foolishly married again very quickly, and I started having the same problems again.

My husband and I decided to get a fresh start by moving to Phoenix, Arizona. When that didn't work out, we decided to move back to my home town of Kansas City — the very place I had sworn never to return to. I went back there because I needed my mother. She adored my son and helped me immensely in caring for him.

Becoming Desperate

At this point in time, I was so depressed that I started seeking help. I sensed that God had the only answers for me, so I started faithfully attending church and studying the Bible.

I had not been a regular churchgoer since I was a young

teenager at home. I had become too busy. Maybe it just was not the "cool" thing to do. After I went to college, I did not know anyone who bothered to go to church. I considered church to be for the old days — a haven for hypocrites.

But life has a way of getting your attention. I had experienced some major heartaches by the time I returned to church — serious things. I had a son with a potentially life-threatening medical problem that wasn't going away. My subsequent divorce from his dad had rocked his world in a damaging way. My second marriage was in trouble, giving me and my son more emotional pain than I had bargained for.

My second husband and I sought professional counseling, and we were told that there was not much hope of us reconciling our differences. That was not the answer I wanted to hear, but I feared it was right. I was angry and depressed. My stubborn will was set on making the marriage work. I did not want to fail again. My moods swung from resignation to brief periods of hope.

Before long, I decided to ask my church's young pastor to provide me with some professional spiritual counseling. He started me memorizing scripture. One evening, I decided to ask the pastor what it meant to be saved. I knew I was a little fuzzy on the details. He told me what I needed to do, and he asked me to give it serious consideration.

A Night of Surrender

As I drove away from the pastor's office that evening, I was engaged in deep thought about my relationship with God. I thought about my counseling assignments, the new things I was learning and my painful personal problems. My mind was busy trying to grasp it all.

I had gone to my pastor holding on to a shred of hope that God could help my situation. I was pretty much out of ideas for my happiness.

Earlier, I had decided that I should try to read the Bible. I believed in God, and I believed the Bible was God's Word. I grabbed an old Bible my aunt gave me in 1963, and tried to read it. But there were so many problems consuming my mind, I could not follow what I was reading long enough to make sense of it.

I had been praying to God ever since my son's diagnosis in 1977. It had not helped much that I could tell, but I kept praying—just in case it might help. There did not seem to be much choice.

Occasionally, I picked up some free leaflets that were on display at the back of church. They concerned compelling topics, and always each one ended by asking the reader to make a commitment to Jesus. I read through them, and hoped I had said and done all they explained about the way to God.

I thought about those leaflets as I drove home from my counseling session that night. There was a place to sign and date them. I had not done that before because I did not know any specific date I could put down. It was not really clear to me.

I started praying from the time I left my counseling session. I prayed all the way home. Whatever it would take to get right with God, I was ready to do it. I was weary. I was troubled. I had problems that I knew no one on earth could solve. I felt that God was my only solution. I had all I could stand of hurt, disappointment, heartache and depression.

I asked God to direct me if He wanted me to pull the car over and pray about my decision even before I got home. I did not hear any answer or have a feeling, so I kept driving. When I got home, I told my husband what the pastor had shared with me. He said he guessed I had nothing to lose. His comments encouraged me. He did not realize the seriousness of my decision, or the effect my newfound zeal would have on our relationship.

I looked around the house and found and signed those leaflets I had gotten at church. I reviewed what they said about salvation. I knew that I was a sinner and, of course, I was sorry for my sins. I believed in Jesus and wanted him to be my Savior. I signed two of the leaflets just to make sure. I thought, "Oh, what could ink on paper mean?" Still, I wrote my name and the date — September 16, 1983.

In my bed in the dark that night, I kept praying. I had the uneasy feeling that even though I knew and believed the statements of faith in the leaflets, there was something I missed. My heart cried, "I give up. I have made a mess of my life, but I give it to You. If You can do anything with it, it's Yours. I'm not going my way any longer."

I meant that with my whole heart. I sensed it was the most radical thing I had ever done in my life. Hadn't I always admired people with the guts to be radical? My way — my culture's way — had not worked for me. I just had to do something, and I felt signing those leaflets was the right thing.

When I did so, I felt a release. It felt revolutionary, and that was exciting. I was free somehow. I did not understand it. But sometime later a feeling of peace settled over me, and I went to sleep.

The Consequences of Surrender

In the days and weeks after that night, I knew my prayer was heard. Joy began to grow inside me.

First, I noticed people at the hospital where I worked smiling at me. I thought it was strange, because they had not smiled at me before. When I thought that through, I realized it was because I had first smiled at them. The smiles let me know for sure that God had heard, and Jesus was really in my heart.

Somehow, He was giving me a peace and joy that my life

had lacked. The joy that I began to feel was my encouragement that there was a God, and He had heard me. It was the fruit of my pivotal prayer of surrender.

Did my prayer change my marriage? It changed everything in my life, but not in ways I understood. Tension in my marriage did not decrease, and despite all my prayers for our marriage to be healed, God had not change my husband's decision to reject Him.

Also, my son's medical problems were not going away. Frequent hospital stays, medicines, tests and trips to doctors continued.

With my depressive habits and serious nature, the joy I felt was a miracle to me. It was as shiny as a diamond on a black display cloth. It had not come from me. It was from God!

Knowing that God had heard my prayer and was healing the hurt in my heart allowed me a freedom I had never known before. I was different inside. The core of me that was confused and hurting started healing. It was like a big, dark cloud over my head had suddenly dissipated. I did not understand it. I had a lot to learn, and the days ahead weren't going to be easy.

My marriage was broken, but now I had Jesus walking with me. I began to read and understand the Bible. I was committed to going to church and opening my heart to a new way to live.

Two Blessings

I continued to heal and trust God for His leading me in my life's journey. As years went by, I was soon to learn that God had two wonderful surprises in store for me.

The first was a godly husband named Robert Hinds. I met Rob because I was involved in the aviation industry. I had managed to complete my college degree by taking courses in

Robert & Evelyn Hinds

bits and pieces as I could find the time. I then pursued certification as an avionics mechanic. I was licensed in 1988 and went to work for TWA. I was assigned to a facility in Kansas City, and that is where I met Rob.

This time around, I took it slow. I didn't want to get involved with another man who did not share my faith. We dated for a year before we married in 1991. He has proved to be one of my greatest blessings.

The second surprise was a ministry that God entrusted to me. At the time this ministry began, Rob and I had moved to Claremore, Oklahoma, and he was working for American Airlines in nearby Tulsa. I had quit my job and was focusing on church activities.

I had always been an avid reader, and one day I ran across a book titled, *In My Father's House* by Corrie ten Boom.[2] It was all about how Corrie's father had prepared her from childhood to live her life for Jesus and to love the Jewish people. Later, when World War II broke out and the Nazis conquered Holland where the ten Boom family lived, they started hiding Jews in their homes.

Their protection of Jewish people ultimately led to the arrest of the whole family and their deportation to Nazi concentration camps. Corrie was the only one of her family to survive, due to a clerical error that resulted in her early release.

After the war, Corrie began to travel all over the world. She shared her horrible concentration camp experiences and taught the spiritual principles she had learned from them. She became famous when a book about her life was published in 1971. It was titled, *The Hiding Place*.[3] It was followed in 1975 by a movie with the same title.[4]

Corrie's story and her sermons had a profound impact on my life. I just couldn't get her story out of my mind. The result was that in 1997, the women of my church in Claremore asked me to put together a spiritual presentation for them. I got the idea of presenting Corrie's story in dramatic form by dressing like her and presenting the Gospel as she would have done.

I received an overwhelmingly positive response which led me to believe that God had raised up a ministry for me — a ministry which I named, "Arts Touching Hearts." Since that time, I have literally gone all over the world portraying and teaching Corrie's profound biblical insights about trusting and obeying God and practicing forgiveness.

Through seeing and portraying Corrie's life of forgiveness, I learned the forgiveness of my God even more fully.

Conclusion

My messy life is a testimony to God's grace, mercy and lovingkindness. He never gave up on me. Instead, he took a shattered, depressed woman with little hope and spiritually renewed her, and gave her a godly husband. Then He raised up a ministry for her that incorporated talents and gifts He had given her.

My message for you is to never give up hope. Focus your eyes on Jesus and lean hard on Him in faith and repentance — and then, step back and watch in amazement as God begins to perform miracles in your life.[5]

To God be the glory!

Chapter 17

A Jewish Musician

Psalm 105

1) Oh give thanks to Yahweh, call upon His name; make known His acts among the peoples.

2) Sing to Him, sing praises to Him; muse on all His wondrous deeds.

3) Boast in His holy name; let the heart of those who seek Yahweh be glad.

(Marty Goetz is one of the foremost Messianic musicians today. He and his wife, Jennifer, live in Brentwood, Tennessee.[1])

I was born in Cleveland, Ohio, in April of 1952. My parents, Albert and Florence Goetz, were Conservative Jews who were descended from Orthodox parents and grandparents. As a family, we were members of The Temple on the Heights and occasionally attended Shabbat services. We annually worshiped on the "High Holy Days" (for which seats had to be purchased due to the once-a-year crowds). In addition, we always celebrated Hanukkah and Passover in our home or in the home of a family member.

The town of Beachwood, Ohio, in which I grew up was over 90% Jewish, but the surrounding areas were a mix of both Jews and Gentiles. I knew nothing about Christianity and didn't know one Christian from another. To me, there was us, and there was them.

In addition to my public education, I also attended Hebrew school through my elementary and middle school years. On Saturdays, I would go to Sabbath school, learning to read from the Torah in preparation for my Bar Mitzvah. I learned to sing the synagogue service in a boy's chorus called, "The Cantor's Club."

Coming of Age

In April 1965, I celebrated my Bar Mitzvah at Heights Temple. Later in life, I wrote a song called "A Jew Born Anew." In it, I described my coming of age event in these words:[2]

> I had a Bar Mitzvah when I was thirteen
> The greatest Bar Mitzvah that you've ever
> seen.
> The temple on the corner of Mayfield and Lee
> Was filled with my friends and my family.
> All of them proud as proud could be,
> With catering far as the eye could see,
> Complete with a chopped liver statue of me.

None of these religious activities produced in me a personal knowledge of God. When I was a child, those whom I believed did have a knowledge of God, such as my Polish-born Orthodox great grandfather, were somewhat imposing and even intimidating figures. They wore black coats, had long beards and followed a strict religious code.

Once my formal Jewish education was complete, I followed the path of many of my generation by drifting away from religious observances, except for holidays and family traditions.

That being said, one essential aspect of Judaism that stayed with me was the chanting of prayers and the music in the synagogue, along with secular Hebrew songs such as *Hatikvah* (Israel's national anthem) which were hauntingly beautiful and affected me in a deeply personal way.

By the time I was in high school, after years of piano lessons, I played the electric organ in rock and roll bands. I loved playing, but I couldn't stand loud music, fearing it would damage my hearing. When we would practice or play a job, scarce as they were, I would often stuff cotton in my ears! Though I never became a rock musician, those years of playing songs "by ear" prepared me for a future in music.

Off to College

In 1970, after my graduation from high school, I headed to Carnegie-Mellon University in Pittsburgh to major in English. There, I met a fellow named Bert Lloyd who was a talented singer. We formed a musical team called, "Bert & Marty," and we began entertaining in local clubs and cabarets. By the time I graduated in 1974, I had been badly bitten by the show business bug.

We decided to try for the "big time," so we moved to New York City and hired an agent who promptly booked us into a resort hotel in the Catskill Mountains, about 100 miles north of New York City.

This beautiful area served as the summer resort for thousands of East Coast Jews. It was referred to as "The Borscht Belt." Our first summer there, we were selected as the "Best New Act." During the rest of each year we were together, we lived in Manhattan and performed at various clubs.

Things were really going great for us until Bert, who was a Methodist, decided to get more serious about his faith. He started attending a Pentecostal congregation called, The Rock Church. Soon after, he proclaimed that he had been "born-again." I had little idea what that meant, but it definitely produced a change in him. He started attending church regularly and began handing out tracts and preaching about Jesus.

Bert seemed to care more about Jesus than about "Bert & Marty."

Marty Goetz

Bert was a great guy, and I loved him, but I was provoked by his personal commitment to this man named Jesus and his expressed desire for me to believe in Him too. What I tried to make him understand was that Jews just don't believe in Jesus.

A Crucial Decision

My internal conflicts eventually led me to initiate the breakup of "Bert & Marty." I spent the next couple of years playing in restaurants and piano bars, achieving some measure of success and gaining a considerable following. In addition, my cousin and I were writing some really good songs, which we both hoped would lead to a recording contract.

In pursuit of this dream, in January of 1978, I decided to move to Los Angeles. En route to California, I stopped by my parents' house in Ohio for a brief visit. While I was there, I found on their bookshelf one of those big "Family Bibles." What they were doing with it, I had no idea. I thought they must have won it in some sweepstakes contest.

I took the Bible with me in my backpack because I wanted to find out more about this Jesus with whom Bert and his friends were so obsessed.

Once I arrived in Los Angeles, I spent my mornings peddling my songs. In the afternoons, I would read my Family Bible, featuring a full-page portrait of a solemn looking Jesus.

I began my reading of the New Testament with the Book of Matthew, and I was immediately struck by the first two lines. They read, "The book of the genealogy of Jesus Christ, the son of David, the son of Abraham." I thought, "Wow! That's strange. I know about those people. I'm reading about Jesus Christ and all these people are Jewish!" I knew because I had heard about them in Hebrew school.

The more I read, the more I realized that Jesus was a Jew. As a matter of fact, He seemed to me to be more Jewish than I was! Until that moment, I had seen Him as nothing more than a dead man on a cross.

Suddenly, Jesus began to come alive to me, and I wondered if He could be my Messiah — the Messiah for whom my people had been waiting for so long.

A More Crucial Decision

The Lord was obviously preparing my heart for what happened next. I was visiting one evening with a girl who was a friend of Bert's and who had been praying for me for a long time. She suddenly told me she had to go to a Bible study. She asked me to stay and watch her apartment, and I agreed.

After she left, I went out on her balcony that overlooked the Sunset Strip. In the distance, I saw what appeared to be a cross illuminated by a bright, white light. (It was actually a large metal telephone pole!) Nonetheless, as I stared at it, I wondered, "Is Jesus after me?"

When my friend returned, I related this experience to her, and she was filled with excitement, telling me that God, indeed, was calling me. Soon after, she invited me to go with her and some friends to a Sunday morning worship service at the beach.

It was like no service I had ever seen, with people sitting on the sand, singing and raising their hands in praise to the Lord. After the music had finished, a man in a sweat suit, obviously the preacher whom people had come to hear, stepped forward. His name was Hal Lindsey.

When Hal finished, he called on a person to come forward and preside over communion. The fellow held up the bread and said, "Baruch atah Adonai, Eloheinu melech haolam, hamotzi lechem min ha-aretz." (Translation: "Blessed are You, O Lord our God, King of the universe, who brings forth bread from the earth.") He then proceeded to say a similar Hebrew prayer over the wine.

By this time, I was thoroughly unsettled, thinking with astonishment, "Oh my! There are Jews here." I did not expect to hear the prayers I had prayed in synagogue spoken on this Southern California beach filled with born-again Christians.

I told my friend, "I've got to get out of here!" I asked her to take me home, and she agreed. I was really shaken up, but as she was driving, she suddenly said, "I'm sorry to tell you this, but I can't take you home right now because I've got to go to a church called The Vineyard." By this time, I didn't know what to think, so I said, "Okay, okay, take me with you."

She took me to a congregation in the San Fernando Valley that was led by a young, fair-haired pastor named Kenn Gulliksen and his wife, Joanie. I experienced another worship service where people were singing with hands raised, just as they did on the beach. I could feel in that room a peace and a presence unlike any I had ever felt. I know now it was the

Holy Spirit.

As the service came to a close, Kenn gave an invitation for people to come to the front of the church and accept Jesus. Somehow, in that moment, I realized I was a sinner in need of a Savior and knew I had to go forward. My friend took my hand and walked with me down the aisle to kneel, along with others, at the steps in front of the altar. Together we said a prayer of repentance, were given a Bible, and were welcomed into the family of God. In that moment of celebration, I couldn't help but thinking, "Oy! How am I going to tell the folks in Cleveland about this?"

That was February 12, 1978. I was 25 years old. A few months later, in April, I was baptized in the Pacific Ocean by Hal Lindsey.

The many prayers of Bert and his friends on my behalf had finally been answered. Like Bert, I was now in love with the One I was to come to know by His Hebrew name — Yeshua.

Sanctification

My sanctification process began with the Holy Spirit stripping away my self-centeredness, pride and ego. He then refocused my musical talents into putting music to Scripture and producing worship songs to the Lord's honor and glory.

I started moving in Christian music circles, and I began traveling around the nation singing in churches, Messianic congregations and conferences. I also began working with major Messianic Jewish ministries like Chosen People, Jewish Voice and Jews for Jesus.

A Major Break

My involvement in The Vineyard led to my making many new friends in this newfound faith. Eventually, these relationships led to my being part of the backup band for Debby Boone, the daughter of Pat Boone. Debby had recently had a huge hit record titled, "You Light Up My Life."

I soon became her musical conductor and traveled with her for over a decade. She also recorded some of my compositions, including my first, "The Twenty-Third Psalm." This opportunity opened doors for me all over the country and even the world.

Along the way, I met and was embraced by other Jewish believers in Jesus, which led to my becoming a voice in what is known as the Messianic Movement.

A Godly Wife

I met Jennifer, the woman who would become my wife, in 1981, at the wedding of a mutual friend. I had seen her the night before at a Jews for Jesus meeting at The Vineyard. When, at the wedding, I introduced myself to her, she told me her name was Jennifer Yaffee. Seeing a perplexed look on my face at the sound of her last name, she declared, "I'm Jewish."

I knew at that moment I had bumped into someone very special. It took me over three and a half years to muster up the courage to propose to her, but I finally did — and on November 24, 1984, we were married.

Jennifer had moved to Los Angeles in 1976 and had become a believer in 1979, a year after me. She also came to faith at The Vineyard.

Before we met, she had traveled the world with her boyfriend who was a musician in Bob Dylan's band. Dylan was on a concert tour called, "The Rolling Thunder Revue." She and her boyfriend, together with Dylan, all became believers in Jesus around the same time.

Truly the Lord is an excellent matchmaker. God has blessed us with one daughter, Misha, and she and her husband have given us three precious grandchildren.

Marty and Jennifer Goetz

Conclusion

Life in Yeshua has been, for me, an undeserved, uninterrupted, and unmitigated blessing — but it has not been without its challenges. Because of deep-rooted historical anti-Semitism, often coming through the Church, a Jew "coming to Christ" is often viewed as having abandoned his own people to become, for lack of a better word, a "traitor" to the faith of his fathers. This is particularly true among the Orthodox, where a child who "converts to Christianity" might even be declared "dead."

In the Jewish community in which I was raised, such radical steps were not taken, However my family and friends were, to say the least, not pleased with the decision I had made. Thus, in my song, "A Jew Born Anew," which I quoted earlier, the second stanza reflects the change in attitude toward me once I accepted Yeshua:[3]

> Now they ask me how I could go so wrong,
> And why all of a sudden I'm singing this song.

They say "Son you're deserting your fathers
of old,
So why don't you just come back to the fold?
You're such a nice boy or weren't you told
That when you were born they broke the mold.
So whaddya need with this stuff ya been sold?"

The next two verses of the song present my response:

But it's a far, far better thing that I do,
Than I have ever done,
When I believed what they said was true
That Yeshua is God's only son.
Well I've done many things and I don't do a few
But this one thing I do makes Me a Jew Born
Anew,
Yes, through and through I'm a Jew Born Anew

So Hallelujah to Yeshua
From a Jew who never knew ya
Could come to die for a schmo like I was,
Just so I could win the prize
and be with my Messiah in the skies!

My parents, despite their disappointment in the path I had chosen, continued to love and support me, even attending many of my concerts through the years with a combination of pride and embarrassment. I will always be grateful to them for that.

A Final Thought

Regarding the Jewish people, — my people — I pray to have the heart of a man named Saul of Tarsus, better known as the Apostle Paul, who wrote: "I have great sorrow and unceasing grief in my heart. For I could wish that I myself were accursed, separated from Christ for the sake of my brothers, my kinsmen according to the flesh" (Romans 9:2-3).

Or, as he puts it in another passage, "Brethren my heart's

desire and prayer for Israel is that they may be saved" (Romans 10:1, NKJV).

During the days left to Jenny and me on this earth, our constant and fervent desire is that the Lord will continue to work through us and our ministry to share Yeshua with the world.

Just as the Lord worked in my life through the prayers of Bert and his friends for me, we pray He will work through us to cause our fellow Jews, along with many others, to fall in love with Yeshua HaMashiach, the Messiah of Israel and Lord of all![4]

J. C. Ryle

“In justification, the word to be addressed is believe — only believe. In sanctification, the word must be ‘watch, pray and fight.”

(J. C. Ryle, 1816-1900, was an English evangelical Anglican bishop. He was the first Anglican bishop of Liverpool.)

Chapter 18

A Former Nun

"But when He, the Spirit of truth, comes,
He will guide you into all the truth;
for He will not speak from Himself,
but whatever He hears, He will speak;
and He will disclose to you what is to come."
(John 16:13)

(Janet Kinder lives in Dallas, Texas. She speaks to groups about what it means to have a personal relationship with Jesus.)

I was born in St. Louis, Missouri, in September of 1938. I grew up in that city, attending the Catholic Church and going to Catholic schools in the 1940s and 50s. Being raised in that environment, the nuns were my role models. We were taught there were three vocations: religious life, married life and single life.

I perceived the best thing you could do was the religious life since that meant total dedication to God. We were also taught that the way we would know if we had a religious vocation is that there would be signs along the way that would point us to that vocation.

Directional Signs

The first of those signs I remember occurred when I was 16. I felt moved to visit a hospital staffed by Dominican nuns to speak with them about entering their community after high school.

However, by the time I graduated from high school I had

met the love of life (or so I thought). He went off to college to study to become a doctor. As so often happens in these situations, the letters from him became fewer and farther apart.

By that time I was 21, and since I had seriously considered entering the religious life prior to meeting him, I thought that his loss of interest in me must surely be a sign that I had a calling of vocation to religious life.

So, in 1959, on New Year's Eve, I entered the Maryknoll Missionary Novitiate in St. Louis, Missouri. After completing the Novitiate there, I was sent to the Motherhouse in Ossining, New York (the city where the infamous Sing Sing Prison is located). After six and a half years, I came to understand I didn't truly have a religious vocation.

Return to Secular Life

In June of 1966, after moving back to St. Louis and starting to work for TWA as a reservationist, it became apparent to me that it is almost impossible to start living at home (with parents) after being away for so long. Therefore, I moved to Washington D.C., where a friend I knew from the convent was now living. She needed a roommate. Neither of us could afford to live on our own.

God's hand was at work in this situation. I met my first husband, Harold, a few months after arriving in D.C. In 1968, we were married. We were blessed with two children, a boy and a girl. In 1985, Harold died of Hodgkin's Disease. Our children were 12 and 14 at the time.

After being a widow for six and a half years, I met Garry, a wonderful godly man — a strong Christian who had taught a Bible Study for 38 years. He had been a widower for a few years. After about a year and a half of getting to know each other, we were married in 1992.

As we all know, time goes by and takes its toll. In January

2019, it became necessary for Garry to go to a memory care facility. He died in 2023. That brings us up to the present time.

A Life-Impacting Poem

In 1962, while I was still in the convent, I came across the poem, "The Hound of Heaven." I can remember sitting in a lawn chair reading it and weeping profusely. It still makes me cry to this day. It was written by an Englishman, Francis Thompson, in 1893.[1] It is the story of how he spent his life running from God, but God, like a hound relentlessly pursued him.

Well, I was not running from God. However, I did not have a personal relationship with Him or understand the true message of the Gospel. At that time, I thought salvation was the result of how "good" I was. This is known as "works salvation."

When I started thinking back over my life in more detail, I saw there were many times from childhood when God was trying to open my eyes to the truth of the Gospel. I think of those times as "cracks" that let the light of truth into my heart.

Spiritual "Cracks"

The first crack took place when I was about 15. During the summers I had a job working on a Mississippi excursion boat. It was such fun. One of the girls I worked with, Sandy, was from Illinois. She was a Baptist. From time to time, she would say to me, "Janet, are you saved?" It would drive me crazy. I would say, "Sandy, stop asking me something I can't answer. When I die, if I go to Heaven, then I'm saved. I can't answer you until it's over!" Out of the mouths of babes! Actually, that about sums up Catholic doctrine as I understood it.

The second crack came while I was in the convent. In 1962, Pope John XXIII convened the Second Vatican Council. He said he wanted to open the windows and let in fresh air. He certainly did. That is when the Mass started being said in English instead of Latin, and many other changes were made. One change that impacted my life directly was the decision to permit Catholics to read books other than those officially approved by the Church. When I was growing up, we could not read a book unless it had the Imprimatur (seal of approval) of the Catholic Church.

This decision soon impacted me, due to the fact that we had a practice in the convent to have someone read to us while we were eating. In 1964, we started listening to a biography of the life of Martin Luther,

At that time, I knew nothing about the Reformation. My knowledge extended to the fact that during the Middle Ages corruption had crept into the Church in the form of the sale of indulgences.

For those of you who are not familiar with the term "indulgence," according to Catholic doctrine, it is "a way to reduce the amount of punishment one has to undergo for sins." The recipient of an indulgence must perform an action to receive it. After you confess your sins, the priest gives the person a penance, like saying some prayers; then he will give absolution.

Well, during the Middle Ages, to receive an indulgence a person would have to pay a certain sum of money. The church began selling indulgences. That corruption was eventually reformed. I thought that was what the Reformation was about.

When the book about Luther was being read, it focused on the day in October 1517, when Luther nailed his 95 Theses to the church door in Wittenberg, Germany. This was a list of grievances against the Catholic Church. The book mentioned that Luther emphasized that salvation was by grace through faith and not by works. To sustain his position, he quoted two verses from Ephesians 2:

> 8) For by grace you have been saved through faith, and this not of yourselves, it is the gift of God;
>
> 9) not of works, so that no one may boast.

I was eating a bowl of soup and my spoon stopped in mid-air. The thought came to me, "He was right!" I wondered if I had been alive at the time, would I have had enough spiritual insight to realize that truth, or would I have thought he was a heretic?

However, despite this new insight, I did not actually leave the convent until two years later. But, the experience made me begin to realize that the Catholic Church did not teach the biblical truth that through Jesus we have the assurance of our salvation.

The third crack, the one that opened the floodgates, happened in March 1981. In the late 1970s my sister, Joan, joined a Charismatic church. She began sending tapes of the preaching and music. The music was especially inspirational. My first husband and I would listen to the sermons each night when we went to bed.

One day Joan told me about a book she wanted me to read. The title was: *Telling Yourself the Truth* by William Backus and Marie Chapman.[2] It was about how important our self-talk is. The authors advocated that we should get in the habit of telling ourselves the truth. For example, "I am a child of God. He loves me." Thus, instead of saying things like, "Nobody loves me," we should verbally confirm that God loves us.

I went to a Christian bookstore to get the book. On the way out, a book on a display stand caught my eye. It had a huge oil well explosion on the cover. It was *Armageddon and the Middle East Crisis* by John Walvoord.[3] I purchased it that

Janet Kinder

day. The next day I was in my bedroom reading it, and it started talking about the Rapture. Having been raised Catholic, I knew nothing about the Rapture (Catholics do not teach that).

What I had been taught is that when you die you go to Heaven or Hell (maybe Purgatory) depending on how you lived your life. When I read that one day Jesus would appear and take believers up to meet Him in the air, I was thrilled. The biblical reference was 1 Thessalonians 4:

> 16) For the Lord Himself will descend from heaven with a shout, with the voice of the archangel and with the trumpet of God, and the dead in Christ will rise first.
>
> 17) Then we who are alive and remain will be caught up together with them in the clouds to meet the Lord in the air, and so we shall always be with the Lord.
>
> 18) Therefore comfort one another with these

words.

Salvation at Last!

The thought went through my mind: "I wonder what I would have to do to be taken up?" Thankfully, I heard what I thought and said, to myself: "Oh, my goodness! Do I still think that way? Am I still thinking about earning my salvation?"

It was then, on that day in March 1981, there in my bedroom, that I got on my knees and asked Jesus to forgive me of my sins and become my Savior and Lord — and He did, and He is!

It was an incredible moment of surrender. It was as if I could hear angels shouting, "Alleluia! She got it! She finally got it!" The second thought was, I'll bet Sandy (my friend from the excursion boat) has been praying for me all these years!"

That thought about Sandy brings me to further evidence of how amazing God is. By this time in 1981, I was in my forties and had lost touch with Sandy. I prayed and prayed that God would bring us together. I tried several times to find her (remember, this was before the internet). Finally, I turned it over to God and said, "You are going to have to bring us together."

At the time I prayed that prayer, my daughter was working for an oil and gas company, and they had a computer program that located people. Using that program, my daughter was able to locate Sandy. I called and we have been in touch ever since.

To show you what an awesome God we have, at the time I got in touch with Sandy, she was going through a really difficult time. You can imagine how my news lifted her spirits. God knew all this was going to happen way back when we were on the excursion boat.

Final Observations

When we come to know Jesus personally it is not the end, it is the beginning. Jesus continues to pursue us and lead us continually to a more personal and intimate relationship with Him.

So, here it was March 1981, and I'm born again, and I am going to live happily ever after — well, not quite. I will of course one day, but not just yet. Revelation chapter 21 tells us:

> 1) Then I saw a new heaven and a new earth; for the first heaven and the first earth passed away . . .
>
> 3) . . . and God Himself will be among them,
>
> 4) and He will wipe away every tear from their eyes; and there will no longer be any death; there will no longer be any mourning, or crying, or pain. The first things passed away.

But not yet, we are still living in the "first things." My life going forward was like everyone's — a mixture of joys and sorrows.

Joys: After March 1981 our family was led to a truly Bible believing church in Dallas. Also, in 1983, a friend asked me to go to Bible Study Fellowship, a comprehensive Bible Study that focuses on actually studying the Bible.

Sorrows: In August 1988, Harold, my husband of 17½ years, and the father of my children, died.

Joys: In June of 1991 I met Garry, a godly man who was a widower. We were married in 1992.

Sorrow: In 2019, Garry developed Alzheimer's and died in 2023.

After going through sorrow, we know that while none of us want to suffer, when we do so, it causes us to lean harder on Jesus, and when we lean harder, Jesus holds us closer. It may not be happily ever after, but we come to know, "the joy of the Lord is our strength" (Nehemiah 8:10). And as my favorite scripture, says (2 Corinthians 4):

> 16) Therefore we do not lose heart, but though our outer man is decaying, yet our inner man is being renewed day by day.
>
> 17) For our momentary, light affliction is working out for us an eternal weight of glory far beyond all comparison,
>
> 18) while we look not at the things which are seen, but at the things which are not seen; for the things which are seen are temporal, but the things which are not seen are eternal.

Conclusion

In closing, I want to leave you with a thought from my deceased husband, Garry. He would say, "When most people read a book, they will forget what it said. Some may remember it for a day or so. Very few will make notes and take action." He would then emphasize that "a goal without an action plan is nothing but a wish." So here is your action plan:

1) Determine to take time to pray every day.
2) Look back over your life and write your testimony. Then share it with others.
3) Spend time in the Word. It is God's love letter to us. It is what sustains us.
4) Remember, the best is yet to be! In the meantime, if you are going through a difficult time, lean hard on Jesus.

"No matter how many steps you may take away from God, you need to take only one to return."

(Author unknown)

Chapter 19

A Scientist

Colossians 2

> 8) See to it that no one takes you captive through philosophy and empty deception, according to the tradition of men, according to the elementary principles of the world, and not according to Christ.
>
> 9) For in Him all the fullness of Deity dwells bodily . . .

(Dr. James Hugg and his wife, Susan, live in Tyler, Texas, where he serves as a professor of science and mathematics at various Christian schools.)

As a child, my parents taught me and my four younger siblings to believe in Santa Claus, the Easter Bunny, the Tooth Fairy, Jesus and the Bible. When I discovered that Santa Claus, the Easter Bunny and the Tooth Fairy were imaginary, I began to suspect that Jesus and the Bible were make-believe, too.

As I approached adolescence, I read many science books and developed a thoroughly doubtful attitude about the supernatural.

Like Paul, I will engage now in some "foolish" bragging to convince you that I am an authentic scientist. "But whatever gains I had, I counted as loss for the sake of Christ. Indeed, I count everything as loss because of the surpassing worth of knowing Christ Jesus my Lord" (Philippians 3:7-8).

An Overachiever

I was born in Louisiana in 1952, and my family moved to Oklahoma City in 1962. While growing up there, I was an overachiever in everything I put my hand to. Since I quickly learned reading and arithmetic, I skipped over the second grade. I was tested extensively, and my parents were told that my IQ was over 160.

There were no public-school programs for "gifted" kids, and my parents were never able to afford private schools for me, so I simply taught myself as much as I could. For example, we acquired a *World Book Encyclopedia* set, which I systematically read. I also visited the public library weekly to borrow science books.

I was quite active in Scouting. As an overachiever, I rapidly earned the Eagle Scout rank, which required 21 merit badges. Then I added 20 additional merit badges to earn four Eagle Palms.

Rejecting God

As a 12-year-old Boy Scout I earned the God and Country Award, in part by volunteering my service in my family's mainline church. I was also required to interview my pastor about the church's doctrines.

When I did so, the pastor cynically denied the authenticity of the Bible, the divinity of Jesus and the existence of God! His "ministry," he said, was to teach the congregation psychological self-help techniques to cope with life and feel better about themselves! He said the music, prayers and sermons of the church were just to make people feel better.

Today, I would call this pastor a "Christian Atheist" — "having the appearance of godliness but denying its power" (2 Timothy 3:5).

I was 13 when I rejected God, declared myself an Atheist and embraced Evolution as my worldview. My Humanistic textbooks and teachers further convinced me that the Bible was an invention of ruling men who used religion to control uneducated people with weak minds. I frequently quoted Karl Marx who proclaimed, "Religion is the opium of the people."

I was taught and gullibly believed that the Bible is full of mythology, superstition and contradictions — a compilation of legends adapted from many cultures. In high school I aggressively ridiculed Christians and persecuted them for believing what I thought was imaginary nonsense.

More Overachievement

One of my talents was music. In High School, I played the French Horn for both orchestra and marching band. I was first chair French Horn in the high school orchestra and won a seat on the Oklahoma City Junior Symphony. I played trumpet in the Pep Band (football and basketball games). I was the marching band Drum Major. Then, as a junior, I joined the state-champion chorus ("Cry-Slurs") at our large (3600 students) high school and became the president and the principal male soloist in my senior year.

I competed successfully in high school debate and oratory tournaments, winning first place trophies in both categories. I delivered a dramatic (although mocking) rendition of Jonathan Edward's famous sermon "Sinners in the Hands of an Angry God," earning for myself the facetious nickname "Reverend."

I was accepted for early admission (requiring my skipping my senior year of high school) at the California Institute of Technology (Caltech) and Massachusetts Institute of Technology (MIT), but I decided that I was not mature enough to be so far away from home at age 16. I deferred until after high school graduation.

I finally chose to attend Caltech in Pasadena, California, because they had more Nobel prize winners, smaller class sizes and warmer weather. Ironically, the motto of Caltech is "The truth shall set you free," although the quote is never attributed to Jesus (John 8:32). I received a full academic scholarship, which included tuition, room and board, books and fees.

Turning Points

While I was a freshman studying physics at Caltech, a profound event caused me to begin to question my faith in Atheistic Evolution. My father, a petroleum engineer, was killed in a gas-well explosion on my 18th birthday. After his funeral, I began to wonder if there might be life after death and if I might ever see him again.

The second turning point came during my sophomore year. I took a biology course called "Topics in Evolution Theory" taught by Nobel Prize winner Professor Max Delbrück. He revealed in his course that the Theory of Evolution is full of holes, is contradicted by many facts and is based on blind faith in the non-existence of God. He told the class frankly that the Bible offers a better and simpler explanation of the scientific observations related to the origin of life and the universe.

However, he rejected the biblical account simply because of his naturalistic worldview that there was nothing supernatural in the universe. He claimed that no scientist could even entertain the possibility of the supernatural. He expressed his personal faith that natural science would eventually be able to explain the universe as the result of a Big Bang followed by the spontaneous formation of galaxies, planets and life. He believed that all species living and extinct evolved over billions of years guided only by natural selection from random mutations of DNA.

Competing Worldviews

After much soul searching, I rejected Professor Delbrück's claim that a scientist could not consider the possibility of the supernatural. In contrast, I believed that true science pursues truth, wherever that pursuit leads, even to consider the existence of "extraterrestrial" supernatural beings, including God and angels.

As a result of that class in Evolution, I re-examined God and read the whole Bible for the first time. I discovered that many reputable scientists believe that the Bible provides a better explanation of the observed facts of nature about the origin of the universe and life on earth. I also read several outstanding books published by the Institute for Creation Research.[1]

It became clear to me that the order and beauty of the universe demanded a Creator. The two worldviews, Evolution and Creation, are scientific, and both are also religious.

I decided that it takes much more faith to believe in godless Evolution than to believe in the scientifically supported biblical account of Creation by God. I lost faith in Evolution, renounced Atheistic Humanism, and at age 19, accepted God, His Bible and His account of Creation as the truth. I met several Bible-believing scientists at a church in Oklahoma City and, after counseling with them, I was baptized by immersion in water as evidence of my new faith.

Growing in Faith

Over the past five decades, I have continued to seek and find evidence of the truth of God's Word, and my faith in God and His Son, our Messiah, continues to grow. I started studying the Bible in depth and reading from commentaries, especially when I encountered difficult passages. I became very interested in biblical apologetics, which seeks and teaches evidence for the truth of the Bible. I have studied various fields of apologetics, but initially I focused on Creation Science.

I am fully convinced that the Genesis account is true and

more plausibly explains life and the universe than the Theory of Evolution. The plain meaning of the Genesis account conforms with the scientific evidence: God created the universe about 6,000 years ago, caused the worldwide flood (about 2350 BC) and dispersed the post-flood populace from Babel by giving them scores of languages (about 2200 BC). I have found the Bible to be accurate whenever it touches on fields of science, including physics, medicine and archaeology.

Graduate School

I completed my B.S. in Physics and Economics (double major) in three years and decided to stay at Caltech for a fourth year so that I could take a graduate class from Professor Richard Feynman, a Nobel laureate in physics who was noted for being a great teacher. I received an M.S. in Physics after my 4th year at Caltech.

I was admitted to the physics PhD programs at MIT, Stanford University and the University of California at Berkeley. I selected Stanford because I was struck by the beauty and tranquility of its more rural campus, as well as the research opportunities it offered. I was granted a full-academic scholarship including both Teaching and Research Assistantships.

As is typical in physics PhD programs, at the end of the first year of graduate school, a "qualifying exam" is administered. I scored the highest of my grad student cohort of 25 students, so I got the first choice of PhD research projects and chose a nuclear physics experimental/theoretical project.

I completed my PhD in Nuclear Physics with a minor in Electrical Engineering in four years at age 25. I then accepted a position as a research physicist at Shell Exploration and Production Research in Houston, Texas.

While I was a graduate student at Stanford University, I taught an adult Sunday school class on apologetics ("Why Do

We Believe?") and led congregational worship about once each month. I also counseled high-school students in youth camps and weekly youth group meetings. I delivered three sermons at my church about "Reasons to Believe."

First Career – Petroleum Exploration

My job at Shell Research was to increase the accuracy of predicting which subsurface rock formations were filled with water, oil or gas. The overarching goal was energy independence for the USA. I led a team that developed new seismic techniques of exploring for petroleum and field tested them in Oregon, Washington and Alaska.

When that project concluded successfully, I was recruited by British Petroleum in the Dallas area to be manager of their geophysics research department.

Bible Prophecy

In 1981, I first encountered Dr. David Reagan of Lamb & Lion Ministries when he spoke at my church in Houston. I was familiar with many of the fulfilled prophecies associated with the earthly ministry of Jesus. But Dr. Reagan completely blew me away with his clear explanation of future prophecies being fulfilled now or soon. He showed me that the signs of the times indicate that we are living in the season of the Lord's return.

The next year, Dr. Reagan invited me to become a trustee of Lamb & Lion Ministries. I was 29 years old and the youngest person to ever join the Board of Trustees. As of this writing (2024) I am now the longest serving trustee (42 years). I had the honor and responsibility of serving for two years as the chairman of the Board, which is the ministry's traditional term for holding that office.

Jewish Roots

Several times, I visited a Messianic Jewish congregation

(Jews who believe in Jesus) in Dallas. I wondered why I felt an affinity with these Jewish brothers and sisters, so I started to investigate my ancestry.

To my surprise, I uncovered several ancestors who were Jewish believers in Jesus. When they had placed their faith in Yeshua as their Messiah, they apparently dropped all ties to their Jewish heritage, as most Jews did until the mid-20th Century when the first Messianic congregation was founded in Cincinnati, Ohio.[2]

I didn't know what to do with this information, so I just pondered it in my heart until I could gain more insight.

Second Career – Medical Imaging

After a decade in petroleum exploration research, I sought the Lord about a career change and was drawn toward medical imaging. My career in the oil business was essentially about the physics of imaging the earth. Medical imaging is closely related, and I thought people would be much more interesting than rocks!

I started using a local medical library to learn everything I could about MRI (magnetic resonance imaging), and applied for positions at the top research groups. After much prayer, I accepted an offer for an NIH Postdoctoral Fellowship from the University of California at San Francisco where my research focused on stroke and epilepsy.

Meeting My Bride

In San Francisco, I attended Calvary Chapel (founded by Chuck Smith who was featured in the movie "Jesus Revolution"). One Sunday morning I pulled into a parallel parking spot just behind a car that had just parked with a license plate frame proclaiming, "Yeshua is Love in Any Language." A beautiful woman emerged from the car and entered the church building. I ran to meet her. I introduced myself and found out that her name was Susan.

We talked for a while, and discovered that each of us had plans to tour Israel later that Fall. Then, to my consternation, I didn't see Susan again until the following Spring. I found out later that her father (a holocaust survivor) was quite ill, and she had to spend a lot of time with him until he died and went home to see the Lord.

In the meantime, I began to also attend a Messianic Jewish congregation sponsored by Jews for Jesus (the Messianic congregation met on Saturday mornings whereas Calvary Chapel met on Sunday mornings). When it was discovered that I was a singer, I was invited to be part of a worship team

James and Susan Hugg

for a large Jews for Jesus Passover Seder. It included a re-enactment of the Last Supper with detailed explanations of its significance.

At the Passover Seder, I spotted Susan at a table "across the crowded room."[3] The moment the seder was over, I headed straight for Susan with a big smile on my face. We started dating that same week and spent countless hours talking and getting to know each other.

We were in our mid-thirties and realized quickly that we were extremely compatible and very attracted to each other. By June we were engaged, and at the end of September 1990, we married in a Messianic wedding.

Our daughter was born in San Francisco, nine months after our wedding. Our son was born 22 months later after we moved to Detroit.

San Francisco – Detroit – Birmingham

When I finished my NIH Postdoctoral Fellowship, I was notified that I had won the first "Young Investigator Award" of the International Society of Magnetic Resonance Imaging, based on my contribution to the development of new brain MRI techniques that are in use today.

I then accepted a Senior Research Scientist position in the neurology department at Henry Ford Health Science Research Center in Detroit. My own research was focused on stroke. I helped to develop an MRI technique to determine how much of the brain could still be salvaged by rapid intervention.

While in Detroit, we worshiped at a Messianic congregation, and I sang with the worship team. After two brutally cold winters in Michigan, my wife urged me to find work in a warmer climate.

So, we moved to the University of Alabama at Birmingham where I continued my MRI brain research by shifting my focus to epilepsy. We attended a large multi-campus non-denominational church. I also sang on the worship team at a small Messianic congregation.

Israel

In the meantime, I met the cantor and rabbi of the local conservative Jewish congregation in Birmingham, and I expressed an interest in learning to chant the traditional Jewish prayers and the Hebrew scriptures. They were amenable to teaching me. I learned rapidly and we became such good friends that they allowed both Susan and me to perform adult Bat and Bar Mitzvah ceremonies, including chanting from the Torah scroll and offering a short homily. In this way we cemented our connection to the Jewish community.

Since our courtship, Susan and I had been discussing our desire to move to Israel. Susan had strong genealogical evidence of her Jewish heritage, and her father had been a Nazi holocaust survivor. My genealogical evidence was not strong enough to claim Israeli citizenship, but after our adult Bat and Bar Mitzvahs, the rabbi wrote a letter vouching for us.

We decided that our children, ages five and seven, were at good ages to learn Hebrew and we started the application process for "making aliyah" (immigrating into Israel as citizens). In December 1998 we landed in Israel and were granted dual citizenship for the whole family. We spent six months in intensive Hebrew language school in Jerusalem while housed at an "absorption center."

I accepted a job with GE Healthcare, and we moved to a suburb on the Mediterranean bay of Haifa, just 30 miles or so south of Lebanon. We became very active in a Messianic congregation (Tents of Mercy) with a mission to serve Russian-speaking Jews from the former Soviet Union. I sang on the worship team and served as cantor, chanting prayers and the Hebrew Torah readings.

As the senior physicist at GE Healthcare, I helped our team create the first commercial high-field MRI system. Then I transferred into the Functional Imaging Division (also called Nuclear Medicine) as the Physics Department Manager.

We spent seven years in Israel helping our congregation grow from about 100 to 200 people while planting four daughter congregations in the Galilee region.

However, our son was struggling with reading in both Hebrew and English (partially because of dyslexia), so we decided to return to the USA where we could receive more support for his education needs. Besides, Susan had been unable to work as a nurse because the licensing exam was in advanced Hebrew. I requested and received a transfer to the GE Global Research Center (GRC) near Albany, New York.

Albany – Los Angeles – Pittsburgh – Tyler

At GRC I led the commercial development of a new compact digital photon camera that has revolutionized Nuclear Medicine in the last twenty years. This led to my being recruited by a medical technology company in California where I was to serve as Vice President for Research and CTO (Chief Technology Officer).

We moved to the Los Angeles suburbs and became active in a large multi-campus congregation called Shepherd of the Hills, where I counseled junior high and then high school youth, and finally college-age adults as our son matured through those stages.

The company in Los Angeles ended up in bankruptcy, and I took a position with a high tech firm in Pennsylvania. We moved to a suburb of Pittsburgh where we got involved in a rapidly growing church. I served as a high-school counselor and helped start a men's ministry. We were also active in a Messianic congregation where I served as cantor and an elder.

We recently moved to Tyler, Texas, to be near our daughter. I am now teaching a variety of subjects at a Christian high school (chemistry, physics, anatomy and physiology, statistics, calculus and Bible). I also teach physics at a Christian technical university. Thus, I continue "pouring into" young believers, in order to strengthen their faith.

During my years as a research scientist, I have been granted over 25 patents and have more applications still pending. I have published 55 peer-reviewed research papers.

Confidence in God's Word

The contradictions I once thought filled the Bible have evaporated as my understanding of God's Word has grown. I believe that many cultures have borrowed from the truth of the Bible to shape their myths and superstitions.

Most importantly, God has transformed my life and proven to me His existence and His love for His creation. I can see His hand at work daily. I believe the instructions for life given by our Creator God in His Word are the key to a fulfilled life.

I am confident that the remaining Bible prophecies will be fulfilled precisely and completely as the Lord has declared. I am also confident that God's Word is absolute truth from Genesis through Revelation.

Conclusion

God is the Creator and Sustainer of the Universe. He is the loving Father who sent His only Son to be the Savior of His creation.

And He is the Righteous Judge who will one day judge His rebellious creation and send His Son back to Earth as King of kings and Lord of lords to reclaim it and establish a reign of perfect peace, justice and righteousness.

Just as God's Prophetic Word foretold exactly the events surrounding Messiah's first advent, the same Word is clear about His second advent. He will come precisely as He said He would.

The cry of my heart is, ***Maranatha!*** Come quickly, Yeshua! (1 Corinthians 16:22).

Chapter 20

A Cult Member

Matthew 24

4) And Jesus answered and said to them, "See to it that no one deceives you.

5) For many will come in My name, saying, 'I am the Christ,' and will deceive many."

(Jean Eason lives in Lexington, Kentucky, and at age 98 is still active in her ministry to people deceived by cults.)

I was a third generation Jehovah's Witness (JW). When I recall the days of my youth it seems that what I heard most often was, how wrong the "religionists" were in comparison to the JWs, who were right about everything. As a JW, I was concerned with works — not only doing such things as preaching from house to house, but with the things I must not do, such as celebrating the holidays and birthdays.

Every word written by the Watchtower Bible and Tract Society (WBTS) was considered "truth" that must be followed to the letter, whether it was rejecting a blood transfusion, refraining from voting, or refusing to serve in the military. To do otherwise was considered sinning against Jehovah, resulting in the possibility of losing the hope of eternal life.

Developing Doubts

I was married and had three children before I began having serious doubts about the WBTS being God's only channel of communication. These doubts began to emerge when I had to make some very important decisions that simply went against the grain of my personality.

I have in mind things like signing papers to let a baby die rather than take blood. You see, I had an RH factor blood condition and in those days they transfused the baby at birth should a problem occur. Fortunately, I was spared — but I was ready and willing to let my children die! Why? Because I was convinced that the WBTS had the "truth" and should I do differently, I would lose the hope of eternal life and so would my child, should death occur. I developed further doubts when the WBTS got "new light" (additions or changes to what had been previously taught).

On one occasion, the "new light" revealed, that if you see JWs sinning and do not report the person, then you are guilty of that sin yourself. Shortly after this new light came, a sister in our congregation took blood when she hemorrhaged at childbirth. My options were either to report her or have the sin fall on me. Both options bothered me! But you see, when you have no personal relationship with Jesus, you follow people blindly, trusting them to be in God's will. Like a good JW, I reported her and she had to appear before a disciplinary court of elders.

This, along with other "new light" caused me to start thinking about where and how the *Watchtower* authors get their new light! I inherited a WBTS library from one of my relatives, and began reading the older publications. I learned they had changed their interpretation of Scripture many times.

I took note that the modern literature often quoted from the older publications. Now I was able to pick up the very book they quoted from – and guess what? I discovered they often misquoted their own writings, or else took them out of context — and misapplied them. After two years of research, I realized I was following a supposedly infallible organization that was based upon the constantly changing opinions of men.

I thought it interesting that I had never read in current

literature that they had once taught that Jesus was enthroned in 1874 and the earthly phase of the kingdom was to begin in 1914. This was taught during the time my grandfather was a Witness but he had never mentioned it.

How My Ancestors Became Involved With the Jehovah's Witnesses

My Mom's father was a Methodist Sunday School Superintendent in the 1890s when he heard that his cousin had lost his mind. It seemed this cousin was telling everyone that the end of the world was coming in 1914! Grandpa rode his horse over for a visit and found him sane, but somewhat confused. He was reading literature written by Charles T. Russell, the first president of the Watchtower Bible and Tract Society. (Russell believed that God had revealed the only accurate understanding of the Bible to him).

Until this time, Grandpa had been a typical Methodist Christian, with a wife and seven children. He was a very loving, kind gentleman with no bad habits and was a respected farmer in the community. Like most Christians, he believed the salvation plan of the Bible was the acceptance of Jesus Christ.

Grandpa was fascinated with Russell's books. They seemed to be so biblically based, and they were interpreting the Bible in such a way that really excited Grandpa. These beliefs were new to him! They taught that Christ was enthroned in heaven invisibly in 1874 (the second coming of Christ) and the Gentile times would end in 1914, at which time the earthly kingdom would begin under the rule of two heavenly classes residing with God and Christ.

The central doctrine was that the ransom sacrifice of Jesus covered all mankind from Adam until the present time. Grandpa was pleased with the idea that everyone living on the earth (including all those resurrected) would live in a world of righteousness, not being judged until the end of the

Millennium. To grandpa, this was true justice! Grandpa accepted this teaching as well as the work ethics that went along with it.

Grandpa accepted Russell's teachings to be the absolute "truth" of God's Word, and was baptized around 1900. After resigning as Sunday School Superintendent, he left his church to become what he thought was a foot-step follower of Jesus Christ, to proclaim these "truths" to everyone by selling Russell's books for a donation. He felt a great urgency to reach as many as possible before the setting up of God's kingdom on earth, in 1914. All those accepting these teachings would live forever in Heaven.

Attitudes Toward Other Churches

Grandpa and his cousin built a tabernacle and preached to large crowds. He held meetings in his little country home regularly. He allowed his children to continue attending church, but told them not to join since the preachers didn't have the "truth."

Although Russell did not believe other churches had the truth, he didn't seem to hate them as did the succeeding president of the Watchtower Society, J.F. Rutherford, who took control after Russell's death in 1916.

After 1914 came and the JWs were not taken to Heaven as expected, Russell's followers were sadly disappointed. This led to several splits in the organization. One group continued publishing Russell's books. But others rallied around the writings of J.F. Rutherford, who became Russell's successor.

Those who continued to identify with Russell's publications were classified by Rutherford as "the evil slave class." In Rutherford's book, *Vindication* (1931), he had this to say: "The evil slave class claim to be the anointed of God and, these being false, they are therefore 'false Christs.'"[1] In 1931,

Rutherford's group came to be known as "Jehovah's Witnesses." Until then, they were known as "International Bible Students."

Grandpa continued his studies in Watchtower literature. He persisted in distributing these publications in his community. These books started pointing to 1925 as the date for the end of civilization, and when this time passed, other changes began to take place.

Grandpa wrestled with the many important changes and even reversals in doctrine. Since he had totally embraced Watchtower teaching believing that only they had the "truth" — where could he go?

I have childhood memories, of sitting on the front porch with Grandpa and Mom. Their conversation was always interesting. Grandpa truly believed that the prophets of the Old Testament would return just any day. He always quoted the Bible, in an attempt to prove this teaching.

For many years the Witnesses looked forward to the resurrection of the ancient prophets before Armageddon, and that event was always promised to occur "any day now." The Society even built a house and deeded it to Abraham, Isaac and Jacob. When people scoffed at them, they called it persecution and accepted it gladly, arguing that it was evidence that they were true followers of Christ.

Experiencing the Holy Spirit

I stopped attending all JW meetings, and activities, and I entered into a state of spiritual isolation. Where could I go? I had been taught that all other religions were false. Where could I find real truth?

After a great deal of searching, I decided to try out a Christian Church. My husband and I attended for awhile, but we did not come to know the true person of Christ. I remained convinced that churches were of the devil. After all,

I reasoned to myself, churches believe in the concepts of the Trinity, hell fire, and the soul leaving the body at death. I didn't believe any of those doctrines.

While I was trying desperately to sort out all these doctrines, the WBTS got "new light." They issued a new edict that said if any JW attended a Christian church, they would be disfellowshiped. Not knowing whether I was following Satan or Jesus, I submitted to the elders when I was called to a disciplinary meeting. I agreed to stop attending other churches. I was just not yet ready to be disfellowshiped for something I was not yet sure of.

Fifteen years later, my Catholic sister-in-law shared that she was "born again." I'd never heard of a born-again Catholic! But I knew something had happened to her because I saw change in her life. She began giving up bad habits such as smoking. She was aglow with something — I didn't know what. She challenged me to attend one of the meetings, and I went out of curiosity. The speaker shared the love of Jesus in such a way that I'd never heard before. It was obvious his focus was on the personage of Jesus Christ. Oh, how I needed that message! When he finished, he asked that we stand, join hands, and sing the Lord's Prayer.

When we did so, something very unexpected happened. Suddenly, I felt God's liquid love pour over me from the top of my head to the tip of my toes! Without knowing what had happened, I instantly realized I had been searching for the "truth" in all the wrong places.

In John 14:6 Jesus says, "I am the way, the truth and the life, no man comes to the Father except by me." Yes, Jesus is the Truth, and "He was there all the time!" No wonder a song was written by that title. The song, "He Touched Me," came to mind. Now, I understood that, also.

I felt such a joy in my heart. I just wanted to rejoice, but I restrained myself, thinking people would notice a strange look on my face.

When we left, my friend said, "How did you like it?" I just started laughing. I couldn't restrain the joy any longer! She said, "Something happened to you, didn't it?" I replied, "Yes, I can't explain it, but I feel as though I've been cleansed from head to toe!" I realize now that I was touched by the power of the Holy Spirit. God knew I could never find the "truth" by searching through definitions of words. I had my Watchtower blinders on. I couldn't believe the simple Gospel — I had to experience it!

Now, I understood why Paul had to be knocked from his horse to become a believer — some of us are just like that! I thought for sure my new-found joy would be gone the next morning, but it wasn't! I woke up anxious to read the Bible and pray!

As I read through the book of John, I wondered when the word, Jesus, was added to so many pages. I had never before noticed how the Scriptures focused on Him.

Making a Dangerous Promise

I got on my knees, and in the privacy of my living room, I asked Jesus to come into my life. I promised I would do anything He asked of me. (Don't ever pray that prayer if you're not willing to be obedient.) I had no idea what He had in store for me.

My husband liked the change in me, so he was willing to visit prayer meetings and, finally, even church. We were subsequently visited by two JW elders who told us we were going to be disfellowshiped. Think of that — disfellowshiped after 15 years of non-attendance! We were okay as non-attenders, until we started attending a Christian church!

My husband also decided to accept Jesus as his Lord and Savior. The next year was spent in deprogramming ourselves. We had to learn everything over! Meanwhile, we were

Jean Eason

completely ostracized by family and friends.

Call to Ministry

Then the Lord put it in my heart to write a book about my spiritual pilgrimage.[2] After it was published, I was invited to appear on national television along with three other former JWs. Soon, all of us began receiving a ton of mail! I had not expected to go into ministry any more than I had expected to write a book — but here I was, living out the promise: "I'll do anything!"

Before I knew it, I was sharing my research and my newly learned orthodox views with hundreds of JWs and Christians who needed to help loved ones in the JWs. I became a Christian discipler over night, and discovered that my JW discipling skills came in handy!

I feel so very privileged to be called of the Lord to share Jesus with JWs who have been deceived into believing in a false Jesus — whom they identify as the Archangel Michael.

I continue ministering to those ensnared in the cults. I also feel a call to educate Christians about the dangers of the cults. Additionally, Christians need in-depth instructions as to why they believe what they believe. Keep in mind that *Christians convert unbelievers whereas the cults convert Christians.*

At the age of 83, I felt the Lord prompting me to write another book titled, *Bird's-Eye View of the Bible.*[3] He gave me the help I needed to complete a simple book explaining the elementary doctrines of the Bible. My co-author and I were invited to appear on a national televison program. I had not planned this anymore than I had planned all of the other actives I've been engaged in.

Conclusion

Since that time, I have recorded many radio programs, and I'm still invited to speak occasionally. I have never asked to speak but have been invited to speak in over 50 churches as well as conferences, seminaries and colleges.

The Lord has blessed me and my family in a mighty way! My children and six grandchildren are all Christians. As I write this, I am 98 years old. My husband, Bill, and I were married for 74 years before he was called home to the Lord in 2021.

I am very happy in a spiritually strong church in Lexington, Kentucky. I encourage all Education Ministers to teach their members the concept of the Trinity and include a teaching on the cults so members of their congregations can defend their faith against the false gospels.

John Owen

"The growth of trees and plants takes place so slowly that it is not easily seen. Daily we notice little change. But, in course of time, we see that a great change has taken place. So it is with grace. Sanctification is a progressive, lifelong work (Proverbs 4:18). It is an amazing work of God's grace and it is a work to be prayed for (Romans 8:27)."

(John Owen, 1616-1683, as an English Puritan Non-conformist church leader, theologian, and academic administrator at the University of Oxford.)

Chapter 21

A Homeless Wino

Psalm 103

> 1) Bless Yahweh, O my soul, and all that is within me, bless His holy name.
>
> 4) Who redeems your life from the pit, who crowns you with lovingkindness and compassion.
>
> 5) Who satisfies your years with good things, so that your youth is renewed like the eagle.

Jack Hollingsworth was born in Mississippi in 1947. He was the fourth of six children. He died in November of 2017 at the age of 70.

His dad had a good job at a sawmill, but he was an alcoholic, and like most alcoholic families, they moved a lot — mainly when the rent was due.

A Tragic Accident

When Jack was about 6 years old, his daddy was bathing the kids one night. He called for Jack. But before Jack got into the tub, he climbed up on an unlit space heater to get a drink from the sink. The heater turned over. His dad uprighted it and continued with the baths.

What no one knew was that the gas hose to the heater had been knocked loose. This was before the time when they started adding an odor to the gas in Mississippi.

Early the next morning, Jack's dad got up and went to the

bathroom to get ready for work. When he struck a match to light a cigarette, the room exploded, and he was killed.

A New Dad

Jack's mother remarried almost immediately to another alcoholic who also was a sadistic bully. He beat the children unmercifully, particularly Jack.

Despite the fact that he was a drunk and a cruel child abuser, he insisted on reading the Bible to the family every night. And, if anyone of them dozed off or got fidgety, he would beat them while yelling that God was mad at them. Jack decided early on that he wanted nothing to do with such a God.

Jack's stepfather was also a psychological abuser. He called Jack all sorts of demeaning names and constantly belittled him by telling him he was worthless and would never amount to anything.

Needless to say, Jack developed an intense hatred for his stepfather. But he also grew to hate his mother because she refused to intervene to protect him or any of the other children.

One thing sorely missing in Jack's youth was any encouragement. The only encouragement Jack received from anyone while he was growing up came from his music teachers at school who complimented him on his singing.

Two Discoveries

In his teens, Jack made two life-changing discoveries. The first one came when he was 15.

He went on an overnight camping trip with some friends. One of them brought along some beers. Jack tasted one and hated it, but didn't want to admit it. So, he continued drinking, and by the time he had finished his third, he had decided that he had made the greatest discovery of his life. As he put it, he felt like "Superman."

Jack's second discovery came when he turned 17. He and his stepfather got into an argument, and when the man shoved him, Jack suddenly exploded. His resentment of all the years of abuse surfaced, and Jack slugged his stepfather and knocked him across the kitchen. When his stepfather got up, he took off running out the back door. That's when Jack realized that, like most bullies, his stepfather was a coward, and Jack no longer feared him.

The Descent into Darkness

After graduating from high school in 1965, Jack's drinking magnified, as did his involvement in fist fights.

He started hanging out in bars, and he found it impossible to keep a job. He ended up in the big city of Memphis where he turned 21, married a waitress and quickly had a son and a daughter. He soon became so hooked on alcohol that he started experiencing blackouts.

Things became so bad that his family finally had him committed to a state mental hospital. He described it as a "den from hell." People were "screaming, screeching, ranting and crying," while others just "sat stone-faced in silence." Some were shackled. Others were "drooling, spitting, cursing, rocking back and forth or pacing constantly."

Jack said he thought to himself, "God, you must really hate me to let me be in here, but that's okay, 'cause I don't think much of You either."

They put him in the A&R Ward. He said he forgot the technical meaning of A&R, but the patients called it the "Alkie & Retard Ward." It was there that Jack discovered a whole new way to get high. That's because each day they gave the patients what they called "Easter Baskets" that were full of multi-colored egg pills. And if the pills failed to subdue them, they were punished with shock treatments!

Family Tragedy

Shortly after Jack was released, his wife, who was pregnant with their third child, was in a bad auto accident and miscarried the baby. Not long after that, she was pregnant again, and the baby was born malformed and died shortly after its birth.

Jack sought solace in the bottle. He was incapable of working anymore. He was constantly in and out of jail and rehab centers. His spiritual emptiness was intensified by the psychologists who counseled him. They told him he could make up his own god, or he could forget about god, or he could be his own god.

Becoming Homeless

His wife divorced him, and in Jack's words, he became a "wino on the streets," drinking aftershave, disinfectants, liniment, and mouthwash — anything he could get his hands on.

Jack started traveling across the country to California and then back across to Florida. In the process, he was arrested many times for pan-handling and loitering. The police often sent him to the mental ward of the local hospital. Jack once told me that he was the only person he knew of who had been officially declared insane in five different states!

Suicide Attempts

During the 20 years that Jack spent wandering around our nation, he tried to commit suicide twice. In both instances he should have died. In both cases, it was a miracle of God that he survived.

The first attempt occurred in Memphis when he jumped from the Mississippi River bridge. He was so drunk that he missed the river and landed instead on some soft mud. Even so, it should have killed him, but it didn't. It broke him up badly, and he faced a long recovery, but he lived.

The second attempt occurred when he drank two pints of rubbing alcohol and chased them with a soda water. He then climbed under a truck and laid down to die. To his surprise, he awoke the next morning. He felt so bad that he wished he were dead, but he had lived. When he climbed out from under the truck, he noticed that it was a Salvation Army truck. Years later, the Lord brought this memory to his mind and emphasized to him that he could not commit suicide because he was under a call of the Lord to salvation.

The Ultimate Life-Changing Discovery

He finally ended up in Lexington, Kentucky. While panhandling there, some people on the street told him, "We don't have any money to give you, but if you will go into the building behind you, you will find some help." Jack did, and he discovered it was a state detox center.

He also discovered a little 4' 10" counselor named Sally. He didn't like her because she was a Yankee from Illinois, she was feisty and he couldn't con her.

In one of their first conversations, she scared him with a word of knowledge from the Lord. She told him that his alcoholism was a manifestation of a deeper problem and that part of that problem was guilt he felt about the death of his father.

Specifically, she said, "Jack, you didn't kill your father. His death was an accident." Jack was dumbfounded by this statement. He had never shared with anyone his deep-seated guilt over his father's death. He concluded that Sally must be a witch, and he decided to have nothing more to do with her.

But he found himself unable to stay away from the detox center. He kept coming back, drawn to Sally like a magnet.

One night she stuck her finger in his face and said, "Jack,

in the name of Jesus, you will never be able to get drunk again." Jack laughed. "Lady," he said, "you are talking to a professional drunk."

Jack left and resumed his drinking. He drank non-stop for a week and could not get a buzz. He finally gave up and returned to the detox center. He sought out Sally and said to her, "Tell me more about this Jesus." She did, and Jack accepted Jesus as his Lord and Savior.

The Day of Salvation

It was December 8, 1988. Jack was 41 years old. The scripture Sally read to him that captured his soul was John 14:6 — "Jesus said, 'I am the Way, the Truth and the Life. No man comes to the Father except by Me.'" As Jack later put it:

> Those words plowed through me like a bulldozer going through a rotten building. My walls of secrecy were demolished. My whole rotten life was exposed and laid bare, and it didn't matter any more. I had come to the end of myself. I was crying, and I didn't care who saw me.

Jack got a Bible and started reading it non-stop. He also got a job and held it for a year — something he had never done before.

A Partnership for the Lord

One day Jack went to Sally's house and knocked. He yelled, "It's Jack!" Sally yelled back, "Come on in." She was at the kitchen sink washing dishes. Jack said, "You know I have never really liked you, but I think God wants us to get married." Sally agreed. It was 3 pm. By 4:30 they were married.

In 1993, they decided to form Acts 29 Ministries. They

Jack & Sally Hollingsworth

bought a mobile home and took to the road singing, preach ing, teaching, counseling and praying. They lived on faith from the get-go, and the Lord provided, although He often took them to the end of their rope.

An Incredible Transformation

The Lord had instantly healed Jack of his alcoholism and smoking. He healed his vocal cords and restored his mind. Here's how Jack later described his transformation and renewal:

> The Lord restored my voice and put a song in my heart . . . With His precious, powerful word, He renewed my mind. He healed the relationship with my stepfather and my mother . . . He broke the chains of emotional bondage and established bonds of love and forgiveness.
>
> He delivered me from all the satanic oppression . . . He healed my mental illness and set

> me free. And like the demoniac that Jesus healed and delivered, Jesus told me to go and tell what great things the Lord had done for me.
>
> In less than five years, God undid what the forty years of suffering and destruction had done! God took this hopeless, helpless, wasted street bum and made a singing evangelist out of him!

Second Corinthians 5:17 says, "If anyone is in Christ, he is a new creature; the old things have passed away; behold, new things have come." Jack was a living testimony to the truth of that verse.

Their Ministry

Jack and Sally spent 21 years on the road, traveling for Jesus. They called their ministry, "Acts 29," because they felt like they were taking up where Paul left off at the end of Acts 28.

They lived by faith, and God blessed them, always supplying all their needs. He also worked through them to touch many lives for Jesus as they focused on the homeless, prisoners and alcoholics.

Jack also served as the featured singer on Lamb & Lion Ministry's television program, *Christ in Prophecy.*

Jack spent the final three years of his life caring for his dear wife who had suffered a stroke. He dearly missed his preaching and singing, but he felt, rightfully so, that Sally had to be his primary ministry.

As I look back on Jack's remarkable life —

> I praise God for Jack and Sally Hollingsworth.
>
> I thank God for bringing them into my life.

I praise God that He never gives up on anyone.

I praise God that He is willing to forgive and forget when we place our faith in His Son as our Lord and Savior.

I thank God for the precious memories I have of Jack and Sally.

And I want to shout, "Hallelujah!" every time I think of "Jumping Jack." Jack was given that nickname because he was so full of the joy of the Spirit that he could not sing without jumping and dancing.

Accordingly, I can imagine that right now he is jumping and dancing and singing in Heaven in the presence of the One he loved the most — the Lord Jesus Christ.[1]

Jack singing and dancing.

D. A. Carson

"Some Christians want enough of Christ to be identified with him but not enough to be seriously inconvenienced; they genuinely cling to basic Christian orthodoxy but do not want to engage in serious Bible study; they value moral probity, especially of the public sort, but do not engage in war against inner corruptions; they fret over the quality of the preacher's sermon but do not worry much over the quality of their own prayer life. Such Christians are content with mediocrity."

(D. A. Carson, 1946, is a Canadian evangelical theologian. He is a Distinguished Emeritus Professor of New Testament at the Trinity Evangelical Divinity School and president and co-founder of the Gospel Coalition.)

Chapter 22

A Cultural Christian

Titus 2

> 11) For the grace of God has appeared, bringing salvation to all men,
>
> 12) instructing us that, denying ungodliness and worldly desires, we should live sensibly, righteously, and godly in the present age . . .

(This is Dr. Reagan's personal testimony.)

I spent 20 years running as hard as I could from God.[1] It all began in 1959 when I graduated from the University of Texas. I had gone through college in three years, and I was exhausted. I decided to lay out for a year and work for my dad. I intended to use the time to rest and decide whether I would go to law school or graduate school.

Within a few days after I moved back home, through a bizarre series of circumstances, I found myself serving as the pastor of a little country church in Groesbeck, Texas. I knew then that God was calling me to full time ministry.

But I didn't want to be a minister. I wanted to be a politician. I dreamed of being a governor or serving in the legislature. So I rejected the Lord's call, and I rationalized it by saying, "I'll be a politician for Jesus." In reality, I wanted to be a big shot for Dave Reagan.

Pushing the Lord Aside

I served the little country church for a year and then went off to a Boston graduate school to study international politics.

The school was called The Fletcher School of Law and Diplomacy. It was owned and operated jointly by Tufts and Harvard Universities.

Up to that point in my life I had been greatly blessed. I had been born into a Christian family, raised in the church, received an outstanding education, and fallen in love with a beautiful Christian girl whom I had married.

But when I departed for Fletcher, I began running from the Lord, and my fortunes began to change. I failed to earn my Master's Degree on time because I could not pass the foreign language exam. I had never experienced academic difficulties of any type before in my life, and this failure was a bitter pill. But I was stubborn, and I persisted.

I became one of the first in my class to earn a Doctorate. But I found no satisfaction in this accomplishment. In fact, I hated every moment of it. Writing my 384 page dissertation was pure drudgery to me, so much so that I have looked at it only a couple of times since the day I completed it. It was simply a necessary step in earning a union card for university level teaching — a Doctor's Degree.

Searching for Meaning

I looked forward to teaching with great enthusiasm, believing that it would fill the vacuum I felt so strongly in my soul. But it didn't. I shifted to a career in academic administration. I thought life would take on new meaning if I could only escape the confinement of the classroom. It didn't.

Finally in 1972 I decided to put the academic life behind me and seek the fulfillment of my childhood dreams. I entered politics. I filed to run for Congress and, again, through a bizarre series of circumstances, I ended up as a candidate for the Republican nomination for Governor of Texas! I was only 34 years old. It was a heady experience.

It was also a terribly disillusioning experience. I had always been politically motivated by altruistic considerations. I dreamed of honest government that would serve the needs of the people. I found that most people involved in politics are driven by selfish motives. I had my head in the clouds. I spoke of lofty goals like revising the outdated Texas constitution. I discovered that people were more concerned about dollar-and-cent issues.

Once again I tasted the bitterness of failure. I placed third in a field of seven. I railed against God in my heart. "How could He let me down when I wanted to do so much good in His name?"

Feeling Empty

During the next few years I focused on paying off my campaign debts. I returned to higher education and served as president of one college, dean of another and vice president of a third. I moved almost yearly, giving little consideration to the effect of such a nomadic life upon my wife and two daughters. All that mattered was my career. I was a slave to the sin of ambition.

I achieved a lot in worldly terms. I held prestigious positions. I made a lot of money. But there was no fulfillment. I continued to feel empty inside.

Moving in a New Direction

Then one day I got a brilliant idea. I decided to go into business. My dad was a very successful businessman, and he had urged me for years to get out of the ivory tower and live in the "real world" by starting a business.

It suddenly occurred to me that I could kill two birds with one stone. I could get my earthly father off my back by going into business. At the same time I could get my Heavenly Father off my back by establishing a church-related business. I announced I was going to open a Christian book store and supply center. I thought it was a pure stroke of genius!

My dad wasn't too excited about the type of business I had in mind. He would have preferred something more down-to-earth like a plumbing supply distributorship.

But he encouraged me to take the step. My younger brother was already a successful businessman. Dad felt that at long last there might be some hope for me!

Hoping to Please God

I was more concerned about the reaction of my Heavenly Father because what I wanted more than anything else in the world was inner peace. I knew that could only come from God.

I didn't know anything in those days about how to seek God's will. I just knew God had called me to be a minister, and I figured that He would jump with joy when I finally stopped running away from Him and took one step in His direction, meeting Him halfway, by starting a church-related business.

I was wrong. I was to find out the hard way that God is not interested in our meeting Him halfway. He has gone more than halfway in sending His Son to die for our sins. He expects us to yield fully, not partially, to His will. But I didn't understand that then.

I jumped into the project with great enthusiasm. I believed it had to succeed because it had the blessing of both my physical and spiritual fathers.

Taking the Plunge

I spent a year and a half getting the business set up. I had to find a location, purchase a building, secure the fixtures, review the trade magazines and order the stock.

It was to be the largest Christian store in Dallas — much more than a mere book store. We were going to offer Christian music, Bible school curriculum, religious art, church supplies, choir robes, fiberglass baptistries — you name it.

During the year and a half it took to get the business started, I had no income. My wife and I sold every asset we had, including our house, to generate the money necessary for such a grandiose business.

What we couldn't afford, we secured through loans granted on my dad's credit. It never occurred to me to start small and grow. No, my store had to be the biggest and best.

I called it Renewal House. The name proved prophetic, for God used it to renew me!

I operated the store for a year and a half. Our volume of business grew steadily each month, but never fast enough. There was too much overhead and too much interest on loans.

Finally, the day arrived when I had no operating cash left. I called the bank for more. The answer was "No!"

The Christian Store
established by the author in the 1970s in Dallas, Texas.

Experiencing Failure

I'll never forget that day. Three years of my life — every waking moment — had gone into this project. Now I faced bankruptcy. Failure again. It was more than I could bear. I descended into a pit of depression and became physically ill.

The day finally came when I had to put the "CLOSED" sign on the front door. That was a tough moment. I looked out the window at the homosexual bar that was located right across the street from my store. The place had standing-room-only every night. The money was rolling in. I wanted to scream, "Why me, God? Why not that den of iniquity?"

Just then the owner of the bar drove up in his four-door Jaguar and parked out front. He was wearing an expensive-looking suit. He stood by his car for a moment, lighting a cigar. It was as if Satan was taunting me, saying, "Look how I reward those who serve me!"

The emotional distress intensified later that day when I called the bank to get the total on how much I owed. The answer stunned me: "Your loan balance is $100,000." (That was 1976 when that amount of money had the purchasing power today of $551,000!) One hundred thousand dollars! I could not even imagine that much money. Where would I get it? How could I avoid bankruptcy and total humiliation?

A Limited God

I desperately needed God. But I didn't know how to reach out to Him. I had grown up in a legalistic and sectarian church. We believed we were the only ones who had the truth. We believed the rest of the so-called "Christian world" was terribly deceived. We consigned them to Hell and believed they deserved it because, after all, they didn't agree with us!

We believed the Bible was the Word of God, but we did not believe in the God who was revealed in the Bible. Our God was a "God of Nostalgia." He was the "Grand Old Man in the Sky." He was a God who once performed mighty deeds in Old Testament and New Testament times — but who ran out of gas at the end of the First Century. He had gone into retirement. The age of miracles had ceased.

If I wanted to experience God, I had to go see a movie like *The Ten Commandments,* in Technicolor and Panavision, with a cast of thousands. I would sit there in awe as I witnessed Cecil B. DeMille re-create the miracles of God dividing the Red Sea, leading the Children of Israel with a cloud and feeding them with manna. I would drive home with goose bumps, yearning for such a God today — a God of power who was concerned about me and my problems.

But I didn't believe in such a God. My God was an impersonal God who had more important things to worry about than my problems. Furthermore, even if He were concerned, He couldn't do anything because He no longer intervened in human affairs — except, of course, to bug me to preach!

My church had put God in a box, rejecting His power and setting aside the whole realm of the supernatural. We did not believe in demons or angels. They too had retired at the end of the First Century!

We knew nothing about spiritual warfare. We thought our battle was with flesh and blood. We knew nothing about the power of the Word, the power of prayer or the power of the name of Jesus.

Our faith was all past tense — directed at the Cross. Our faith did not relate to the present or the future. Regarding the present, our attitude was that God had given us a rule book and minds. We were to follow the rules and use our common sense to cope rationally with the problems of life.

Our faith did not relate to the future because we ignored God's Prophetic Word. Also, we were caught up in works salvation, and therefore we were all uncertain about our eternal destiny. The future was unknown. We tried not to think about it.

Living in a Spiritual Vacuum

Our faith was really in our church. We trusted in the

church because we were told that our church was right about everything. We took pride in our church. We took glee in putting down other churches.

We were debaters. We liked to prove that other people were wrong. By age 15 I had pages in the back of my Bible that were designated for every major denominational group. On each page I had a list of proof texts that I used to attack any particular group. We had a zeal to prove we were right about everything.

This was before the days of Christian radio and television and Christian bookstores. Our ministers could keep us in isolation from the rest of the world. We talked only to ourselves.

Religion in Name Only

The point is that as I stood there that day in the mid-1970s facing the chilling reality of a failed business and a $100,000 debt, I had no inner spiritual power to help me cope with the crisis.

Let me take that back. I did have the power, for I had received Jesus as my Savior many years before, and on that day I had received the indwelling power of the Holy Spirit. But I didn't know that. I had never plugged into the power because I had never been taught about it. I had never released the power of the Spirit in my life. Instead, I had stifled and quenched the Spirit.

I could recite the five steps in what our church called "The Plan of Salvation." I could also recite what we called "The Five Acts of Worship." I could give you chapter and verse to substantiate several dozen of our pet doctrines. But I had no power to cope with a business failure and a $100,000 debt.

Wallowing in Self-Pity

So, I did the only thing I knew how to do — I threw a pity party. I wallowed in self-pity. And as I did so, I sank deeper into the pit of depression.

I finally became so despondent that I decided to kill myself. I felt like I just couldn't face the disgrace and pain of such a failure. Also, I was mad at God. How could He let me down so miserably when I had, at long last, deigned to meet Him halfway? In my emotionally perverted reasoning, I decided that by taking my life I would teach God a lesson! I know that sounds weird, but when you are deeply depressed, you don't think too clearly.

For several days I plotted my demise. Just as I had everything carefully planned, I suddenly got an unusual thought: "Why not try God?" That was a strange thought for me because I didn't believe in either a personal or a powerful God. Looking back on it today I can only conclude that the thought must have come from the stirring of the Spirit within me. I had quenched the Spirit, but the Spirit was still there, and He was trying to minister to me in my time of need.

I tried to suppress the thought, but it would not go away. Over and over it came to me: "Why not try God?"

Calling for Help

I finally decided to follow the prompting. I got on the phone and called several friends. I asked them to come to my house. When they arrived, I explained my predicament and asked them to pray for me. One by one they prayed. Their prayers were lifeless and unbelieving. They no more believed in a personal and powerful God than I did.

As the prayers droned on, I became agitated. "This won't do," I interrupted. "None of you are praying with any confidence. You don't understand, I need a miracle! Let's try again and this time, pray with some faith!" I could hardly believe those words came out of my mouth. But they did. My friends started praying again, this time with some fervor.

God performed the miracle the very next morning, and it

transformed my life. You could start guessing right now and guess till the Lord returns, and you would never guess how God answered our prayers.

Being Shaped by God

You see, when God responds to a cry for help, He does so in a manner that is always designed to minister first to the inner man, to the spiritual nature. It's not that He's unconcerned about the physical man and the physical and emotional pain; it's just that His priorities are different from ours. We want to be ministered to from the outside in. He ministers from the inside out, because that is the only kind of ministry that has lasting effects.

If you were to guess how the Lord answered our prayers, you would most likely assume that some man walked in my store the next morning and offered to buy the business for $100,000. That would have been truly remarkable, but it would not have had a transforming effect on me. I would probably have written it off to "coincidence" rather than recognizing it as an answer to prayer. Most likely, I would have sighed with relief and gone on my way continuing to try to meet God halfway.

God answered my prayer miraculously, but He did it in a way designed to get my attention, to convince me that He truly is a personal and powerful God who is on the throne, hears prayers and still performs miracles. He also used a method that was designed to transform me more into the image of His Son.

A Transforming Miracle

Here's what happened. The next morning I went to the store and started calling around trying to find a buyer for my fixtures. I was standing at the front counter talking on the phone when I heard a knock at the front door. I turned and looked at the plate glass door and saw an Asian man and woman standing there. The man was grinning from ear to ear. I pointed to the sign hanging on the door and turned my back on the couple. The sign said, "Closed: Going Out of Business."

The man resumed his knocking. I got mad. Couldn't this fellow read? Why did he have that big grin on his face? The last thing I wanted to see was someone happy. Misery really does love company. I put the phone down, went to the door, opened it about an inch and shouted, "Can't you read? We're closed!"

"Oh yes sir," he replied, "I know you are closed. I'm interested in buying your fixtures."

"Oh!" I replied. "Come in. Come in."

I locked the door and went back to the phone while the Asian man and lady looked around the store. When I finished talking, the man came up to me, still grinning, and said, "Thank you, dear sir, for letting me see your store." He was almost nauseating in his politeness. He continued to grin and started bowing in the Oriental style. Then he started apologizing! "I'm very sorry, dear sir, but you do not have any fixtures I'm interested in. I'm opening up a different type of store."

A Probing Question

I escorted him and the lady to the door. The lady walked out, but as the man got halfway through the door, he suddenly stopped, turned to me and said, "I discern that you are troubled in the spirit. Do you want to talk about it?"

Talk about getting angry! I was livid. Who did this guy think he was? I replied in my "best" Christian manner, "What's it to you?"

"Well," he replied, "I assume from the nature of this store that you must be a Christian. I am too. And I discern that you need ministry. Would you mind if I shared with you what

Jesus Christ has done for me in my life?"

I didn't want to hear his story. I wanted him to leave. But what was I to say? It was like when someone asks if they can pray for you. You may not want them to, but you hate to say no.

"I'm awfully busy," I said, as I glanced at my watch in irritation.

"It won't take but a moment," he replied. He grinned again.

"Okay, okay," I said, "but make it quick."

He turned and said something to the lady in a foreign language, and she left. I locked the door again, and we went to my office. When we sat down on the couch, he put his arm around me and began to pat my shoulder sympathetically. Again, I was outraged. Who does this guy think he is? He hardly knows me, and he has his arm around me!

But I soon forgot my anger as he began to tell his story.

A Fascinating Story

"When I was a small boy, my father came home one day with terror in his eyes. 'The Communists are coming,' he said, 'and they are going to kill us because we are devout Christians.'"

"He told each of us to get two pillow slips and go to the living room. He started running all over the house gathering up items which he piled in the middle of the floor. 'Put these in the pillow slips,' he said, 'and tie the tops.'"

"We were a very wealthy family, but all we took with us that day was what we could stuff into those pillow slips. We fled into the jungle, and we threw ourselves upon the Lord because we didn't know how to survive in the jungle. There were 12 of us in all. We wandered about aimlessly crying out to God to save us."

"Finally, after three weeks, we made it from Hanoi to Saigon, and we rejoiced over the Lord's deliverance."

A Repeat Performance

"We began our life anew. Many years later I came home one day to my family and my aged parents with that same look of terror in my eyes. 'Get the pillow slips,' I yelled. 'The Communists are coming again.'"

"You see, I was a translator at the American Embassy. I had been informed that the Embassy could not arrange for all my family to be flown out. I would not leave without them. So, once again, we had to flee. I knew if we stayed we would be executed because I had worked for the Americans."

"We fled into the Mekong Delta and, again, we began to cry out to God for deliverance. After wandering for several days, we made it to the South China Sea where we discovered a boat full of refugees about to depart. God had saved us a second time!"

"But when the boat got out to sea, it started sinking. There were just too many people on it. Some people panicked and began to push others overboard. Some even threw their children into the sea! We got on our knees and started calling out to God. Soon, a merchant ship appeared and took the survivors on board. God had saved us a third time!"

"We were taken to the Philippines where we were put with thousands of other refugees in a concentration type camp. We began praying that God would give us a new home. A year later the news came that we were being adopted by a Bible Church in Dallas, Texas. God saved us a fourth time."

"So, here we are in a new land starting our lives over. God is so good. He loves us, and He answers our prayers. Lean on Him. He will deliver you."

A Changed Attitude

I looked at the man with tears in my eyes. Before I knew it, I had my arms around him, hugging him in thankfulness for insisting on sharing a story I had not wanted to hear.

When he left, everything had changed. Yet, nothing visible had changed. I still had a failed business. I still owed a bank $100,000. What had changed was me. I no longer felt depressed. I was no longer wallowing in despair and self-pity. I had hope. I knew in my soul that God had heard my prayer and that He had sent that man to assure me that if I would trust in the Lord, everything would turn out all right. God had used an Asian man from halfway around the world to get my eyes off myself and onto His Son.

I had no problems compared to the problems that man had faced. If God could solve his problems, He surely could handle mine. God had finally gotten my attention, but He did not yet have me.

During my years of running from the Lord I had developed many sinful attitudes, thoughts and habits. I was in bondage to pride, ambition and lust. I wrestled daily with a hot temper. I still dreamed of worldly success.

I still had a long way to go before I could become a useful servant of the Lord's. I had to get to know God as a personal, caring and powerful God. I had to get to know myself — to really know myself — by honestly facing up to my faults. I had to learn how to surrender myself to God's will and then how to live on the power of His Spirit rather than the power of my flesh.

Viewing the Bible Differently

The Lord began the process by giving me an insatiable appetite for His Word. I had grown up in a Bible believing church. Theologically we proclaimed the Bible as the revealed Word of God, and we stood on the authority of the

Scriptures. But in practice, we put our traditions above the Word. We played games with Scripture.

When the Word contradicted our doctrines, we either spiritualized the passage or we dispensationalized it. We spiritualized by saying that the passage didn't mean what it said. We dispensationalized by arguing that the passage had ceased to be valid at the end of the First Century.

We also tended to use the Bible as a debating handbook. Rather than reading it to seek truth or simply to allow the Holy Spirit to minister to our hearts, we approached it as though it were the Texas Code Annotated. We looked for proof texts to justify our doctrines and to prove others wrong.

As I started reading the Bible anew, the Spirit led me to read it in a different way. Rather than searching for proof texts, I found myself reading for the sheer joy of it. As I read, I began to make some amazing discoveries. For example, prophecy began to make sense, if I would just believe what it said.

In fact, the whole Bible began to make more sense to me as I began to accept what it said as meaning what it said and as being applicable to me today. As a trained academic, I had always approached the Bible as literature to be analyzed, categorized and theologized. I now became aware that it was written to be believed and acted upon.

It was difficult, but I began to put aside the rationalizing, the spiritualizing and the dispensationalizing. As I did so, I found that the Word began to transform me.

For the first time my eyes were opened to my own faults rather than the faults of others. Time and time again I was brought to my knees in repentance. The Word became a spiritual mirror reflecting my inadequacies compared to the perfection of Jesus.

Seeing God in a New Way

I also began to discover some important things about God. First and foremost was the revelation that "He is the same yesterday, today and forever" (Malachi 3:6 and Hebrews 13:8).

What a discovery that was for me! God had not retired! He is alive and well. He is still the same God as the one revealed in the Bible — a God who is sovereign, personal, loving, caring, powerful and who still intervenes in history in response to the faith of those who seek Him. I could hardly contain my joy.

Tasting the Lord's Discipline

The Word was not my only teacher during those difficult days following my business failure. I was also shaped and molded by the Lord's discipline.

After I sold off all the assets of my business, I still owed the bank $60,000. I negotiated a deal to pay off that debt by agreeing to pay the bank a minimum of $1,000 a month. That obligation meant that my family and I were going to have to learn to live on a greatly reduced income. Our whole lifestyle was transformed almost overnight.

Prior to the business failure, my income had been increasing rapidly almost every year. But like most Americans captivated by Materialism, no matter how much I made, it was not enough. I always needed a bigger house or a larger car. Suddenly, we had to learn how to live a frugal lifestyle. Most of what I earned each month went to pay off the debt. So we mainly lived on my wife's income as a first-grade teacher.

It was the discipline of the Lord. It wasn't easy, but it was another spiritually transforming experience. We were delivered from Materialism. We learned how to live simply, how to count our blessings, how to be satisfied with what we had.

We began to learn about how to trust in the Lord to provide our basic needs.

Playing at Christianity

But we were still pretty much what I would call "Cultural Christians." By that I mean that my wife and I had been born into Christian families, raised in the Church and considered Christian values to be an integral part of our lives. We attended church regularly and made sure that our children were involved in all the church's activities. In short, we were a typical American church-going family.

The problem with that is that we were not committed disciples of the Lord. Like most Christians, we had accepted Jesus as Savior but not as Lord. We had received His Spirit into our lives, but we had never released the power of the Spirit. For me the Spirit was a resident but not president. He resided but He did not preside. My ego was on the throne of my life.

Getting Serious About the Lord

In the years that followed, my sanctification shifted into high gear. I was no longer restrained in developing a personal relationship with Jesus. I began to dispose of all the spiritual garbage I had been taught about God retiring at the end of the First Century. I now believed in the God of the Bible — the sovereign, personal, miracle-working God who still hears prayers and answers them. My guiding verses became two found in 1 Peter 5:

> 6) Therefore humble yourselves under the mighty hand of God, that He may exalt you at the proper time,
>
> 7) casting all your anxiety on Him, because He cares for you.

I began to learn about the Holy Spirit — how He takes up residence inside of Believers and gives them supernatural gifts to serve the Church. I also learned about how He can provide us with guidance and encouragement, if we will only allow Him to do so.

I started being convicted by the Holy Spirit of my un-Christian attitude toward other Believers who were members of different denominations. I learned that all truth is important, but all truth is not equally important. The greatest, foundational truth is that Jesus is Lord. I began to understand that a person who confesses that truth is a brother or sister in Christ regardless of their label as a Baptist or Methodist — or whatever. And I came to realize that it was my duty as a follower of Jesus to love such people rather than condemn them.

I didn't change suddenly and completely overnight. The Spirit was patient with me, but He was determined to shape me more fully into the image of Jesus who had saved me.

Conclusion

My greatest regret is that I wasted 20 years of my life pursuing my ambitions rather than serving the Lord.

I urge you not to make the mistake I did. Don't be a "Cultural Christian" by walking with one foot in the church and the other in the world. Surrender your life fully to the Lord. I will leave your with the words of the Apostle Paul in Romans 12:1 —

> Therefore, I exhort you, brothers, by the mercies of God, to present your bodies as a sacrifice — living, holy and pleasing to God, which is your spiritual service of worship.

Chapter 23

A Summary

1 John 2

> 15) Do not love the world nor the things in the world. If anyone loves the world, the love of the Father is not in him.
>
> 16) For all that is in the world, the lust of the flesh and the lust of the eyes and the boastful pride of life, is not from the Father, but is from the world.
>
> 17) And the world is passing away, and also its lusts, but the one who does the will of God abides forever.

After reading this book, I hope that you now fully understand the quote from Philip Yancey that I provided in the chapter about John Newton: "Grace, like water, always flows downward, to the lowest level." The Apostle Paul put it another way when he observed that "where sin increases, grace abounds all the more" (Romans 5:20-21).

The fundamental message that emerges from the testimonies contained in this book is that there are no sins so dark and depraved that they can permanently separate you from God, if you are willing to repent, cry out to God for forgiveness and accept His Son, Jesus, as your Lord and Savior.

Some people respond to this declaration by pointing out that the Bible says in Matthew 12:31 that there is one unforgivable sin — namely, "blasphemy of the Holy Spirit." But this statement does not contradict what I have said about

God's willingness to forgive any sin through faith in Jesus.

It is the Holy Spirit who witnesses Jesus and draws people to Him, and the rejection of the Spirit's witness of Jesus produces an unforgivable sin unless that rejection is reversed (John 6:40 and John 15:26). And the reason, of course, is there is no salvation whatsoever apart from faith in Jesus (John 14:6).

Biblical Examples

The Bible is filled with examples of God forgiving people of terrible sins in response to their confessions of repentance.

Take King David for example. He is called in the Scriptures "a man after God's own heart" (1 Samuel 13:14). Yet, he was an adulterer and a murderer. But he turned to God with a broken heart for his sins and cried out (Psalm 51):

> 1) Be gracious to me, O God, according to Your lovingkindness; according to the abundance of Your compassion, blot out my transgressions.
>
> 2) Wash me thoroughly from my iniquity, and cleanse me from my sin.

He continued his plea with heart-rending words:

> 10) Create in me a clean heart, O God, and renew a steadfast spirit within me.
>
> 11) Do not cast me away from Your presence, and do not take Your Holy Spirit from me.
>
> 12) Restore to me the joy of Your salvation, and sustain me with a willing spirit.

In the New Testament, we have the example of the Apostle Paul. As I pointed out in Chapter 1, Paul was a zealous Pharisee who viewed the early Christians as apostates of Judaism. He hunted them down, arrested them and oversaw their executions. Yet, God called him, and Paul responded in repentance and faith.

But Paul never forgot the terrible actions he took against the early believers in Jesus:

- "I am the least of the Apostles" (1 Corinthians 15:9).
- "I am the very least of all the saints" (Ephesians 3:8).
- "I am the foremost of sinners" (1Timothy 1:15).
- "Nothing good dwells in me" (Romans 7:18).
- "I am nothing" (2 Corinthians 12:11).

Paul even cried out, "Wretched man that I am; who will deliver me from the body of this death?" Paul then answered his own question by confidently asserting, "Thanks be to God through Jesus Christ our Lord!" (Romans 7:24-25).

And why did he say that? Because he proceeded to declare: "Therefore there is now no condemnation for those who are in Christ Jesus. For the law of the Spirit of life in Christ Jesus has set you free from the law of sin and of death" (Romans 8:1-2).

A Personal Experience

After I finally surrendered my life to Jesus and then was presented with a call to full time ministry, I was traumatized by memories of the sins I had committed during the 20 years I ran from the Lord.

Accordingly, each time I would get up to preach or teach, Satan would start reminding me of my sins by asking, "Who do you think you are to be preaching and teaching the Bible?" The attacks were very painful and left me wondering if God really had called me.

Fortunately, I was delivered from this harassment when the Holy Spirit began reminding me of some very important biblical principles:

- That my sins have been forgiven and forgotten in the sense that they will never be held against me (Jeremiah 31:34 and Hebrews 8:12).
- That my sins have been removed from me "as far as east is from west" (Psalm 103:12).
- That my sins have been "cast into the depths of the seas" (Micah 7:19). And, as Corrie ten Boom used to say, "God has placed a sign there that says, 'No fishing!'"
- That the only people God has to work through are sinners (Romans 3:10-12).

Additionally, one day as Satan was attacking me by reminding me of my past, the Holy Spirit suddenly provided me with a weapon to use against him, based on my knowledge of Bible prophecy. I responded to Satan by reminding him of his future! And he fled like a leopard.

God's Future Judgment of Sin

When Jesus takes the Church (both the living and the dead) out of this world in the Rapture, He is going to judge Believers of their works to determine their degrees of reward. This judgment will be based on the fact that when a person puts their faith in Jesus and are born again, they are given at least one spiritual gift which they are expected to use to advance the Lord's kingdom (1 Corinthians 12:1-11).

But what most Believers do not seem to be aware of is that they will *never* be judged of their sins to determine their eternal destiny. That's because their eternal destiny was determined the moment they placed their faith in Jesus, and their sins were forgiven and forgotten. Hebrews 9:28 tells us that when Jesus "appears a second time for salvation," He will come without reference to sin." That's a "Hallelujah!" verse.

In contrast, those who have never accepted God's marvelous gift of grace in Jesus will be judged of their sins and their works to determine their eternal destiny, and all of them will be condemned to Hell because no one can be saved by their works — even good works (Revelation 20:11-15).

Steve Heitzig, pastor of Calvary Chapel in Albuquerque, New Mexico, has put it this way: "Heaven is not for good people. It is for saved people."[1]

The Signs of the Times

The Bible contains many end-time signs that we are to watch for — signs that will tell us when we are living in the season of the Lord's return. There are many such signs that can be placed into six categories, as follows:

- Signs of Society
- Signs of Nature
- Spiritual Signs
- Signs of Technology
- Signs of World Politics
- Signs of Israel

For the first time in history, all these signs have ***converged***, indicating that we are the terminal generation, and we are thus living on borrowed time.

Mike Gendron, the founder and evangelist for Proclaiming the Gospel Ministry, recently shared a profound insight that shows how close we are to the Lord's return:[2]

> The first 2,000 years of human history ended when the wrath of God was poured out on sin in the Flood.
>
> The second 2,000 years ended when the wrath of God was poured out on sin at the Cross.

> And the third 2,000 years will end with God pouring out His wrath on sin during the Tribulation.

Well, folks, we are at the end of that third 2,000 year period. It's just one more of the many end time signs that are shouting to us from the heavens that Jesus is ready to return.

God is so gracious to give us signs to watch for so that we will know when He is about to pour out His wrath on those who have refused to accept His grace in Jesus.

Conclusion

What about you? Are you ready for the climax of history? Don't take a chance of being left behind to face the horror of the Antichrist after the Rapture occurs. Accept Jesus now as your Lord and Savior in order to be born again and to receive the indwelling power of the Holy Spirit.

Don't hesitate. Do it now, "For God so loved the world, that He gave His only begotten Son, that whoever believes in Him shall not perish, but have eternal life" (John 3:16).

MARANATHA!
(1 Corinthians 16:22)

Resources

Chapter 1: A Zealous Pharisee

No references, except Scripture.

Chapter 2: A Son of Thunder

1) Bibles.net, "Apostle John: How the Son of Thunder Became a Son of God," https://www.bibles.net/apostle-john-son-of-god, page 3.

2) Leah Pittsinger, "John is Transformed by Jesus," https://ministry-to-children.com/forever-changed-lesson-2, page 2.

3) John Stott, *Basic Christianity* (Lisle, Illinois: InterVarsity Press, 1964).

Chapter 3: A Tax Collector

1) James M. Rochford, "Tax Collectors in Jesus' Day," www.eidence unseen.com/theology/historical-theology/tax-collector, page 1.

2) Ibid, page 2.

3) Ibid.

4) GotQuestions.org, "Who was Matthew in the Bible?" www.gotques tions.org/Matthew-in-the-Bible.html, page 2.

5) Mike Leake, "How Much Do We Know About Matthew the Disciple?" www.https://www.biblestudytools.com/bible-study/topical- stud ies/how-much-do-we-know-about-matthew-the-disciple.html, page 2.

6) Wikipedia, "Five Discourses of Matthew," https://en.wikipedia.org/ wiki/Five_Discourses_of_Matthew, pages 2-3.

7) T.C. Schmidt, "Matthew's Literacy as a Tax Collector?" https:// jesusmemoirs.wordpress.com/2019/07/06/the-literacy-of-tax-collec tors, page 1.

Chapter 4: A Slave Trader

1) Jonathan Aitken, *John Newton: From Disgrace to Amazing Grace* (Wheaton, IL: Crossway Books, 2017), page 13.

2) Janet and Geoff Benge, *John Newton: Change of Heart* (Seattle, WA: YWAM Publishers, 2018), page 81.
3) Ibid., page 84.
4) Aitken, page 84.
5) Ibid.
6) Ibid., page 350.
7) Ibid.

Chapter 5: An Oxford Professor

1) There is a myriad of books about C. S. Lewis. Some of the best are as follows:

   Roger Lancelyn Green and Walter Hooper, *C. S. Lewis — A Life: Eccentric Genius, Reluctant Prophet* (Carol Stream, IL: Tyndale House, 2016).

   Beatrice Gormley, *C. S. Lewis: Christian and Storyteller* (Grand Rapids, MI: Eerdmans Books, 1998)

   A. N. Wilson, *C. S. Lewis: A Biography* (New York, NY: W.W. Norton Co., 1990)

   George Sayer, *Jack: A Life of C. S. Lewis* (Wheaton, IL: Crossway, 2005)
2) C. S. Lewis, *Surprised by Joy: The Shape of My Early Life* (London: Fontana Books by William Collins Sons & Co. Ltd, 1959), pages 29-34.
3) Beatrice Gormley, *C. S. Lewis: Christian and Storyteller* (Grand Rapids, MI: Eerdmans Books, 1998), page 34.
4) Lewis, *Surprised by Joy*, page 130.
5) Gormley, page 40.
6) Lewis, *Surprised by Joy,* page 154.
7) Ibid., page 182.
8) Ibid.
9) Gormley, page 86.
10) Lewis, *Surprised by Joy,* page 189.
11) C. S. Lewis, *Mere Christianity* (New York, NY: Macmillan Publishing, 1960), page 56.

Chapter 6: A Jewish Communist

1) Abigail Santamaria, *Joy: Poet, Seeker, and the Woman Who Captivated C. S. Lewis* (New York: Houghton Mifflin Harcourt, 2015), page 33.
2) Lyle W. Dorsett, *And God Came In: The Extraordinary Story of Joy Davidman* (Peabody, Massachusetts: Hendrickson Publishers, first edition in 1983, second edition in 2011), page 60. This is an excellent spiritual biography.
3) Ibid.
4) Santamaria, page 229.
5) Dorsett, page 156.
6) C. S. Lewis, *A Grief Observed*, originally published under the name of N. W. Clerk in 1961 in England by Faber & Faber, Limited. The quotation is found on page 35 of the fourth American edition by The Seabury Press in New York.
7) C. S. Lewis, *Surprised by Joy: The Shape of My Early Life* (London: Harvest Books, 1955), pages 228-229.
8) Lewis, *A Grief Observed*, page 9.
9) Ibid.
10) Ibid., pages 9-10.
11) Ibid., page 27.
12) Ibid., page 38.
13) Ibid., page 42.

Chapter 7: A Ruthless Political Operative

1) Charles W. Colson, *Born Again* (Minneapolis, MN: Chosen Books 2008 revised edition), page 10.
2) Colson, page 10.
3) Ibid., page 32,
4) Ibid.
5) Ibid., page 32.
6) Ibid., page 33.
7) Ibid., page 37.

8) Ibid., page 65.

9) Michael Dobbs, "Charles Colson, Nixon's 'dirty trick" man dies at 80," *The Washington Post*, April 21, 2012, www.washingtonpost.com/politics/whitehouse/chuck-colson-nixons-dirty-tricks-man-dies-at-80/2012/04/21/gIQAaoOHYT_story.html, page 3,

10) Colson, page 65.

11) Ibid,. page 69.

12) Ibid., page 70.

13) Ibid., page 103.

14) Ibid.

15) Dobbs, page 4.

16) Colson, page 34.

17) Ibid., page 142.

18) Wikipedia, "Charles Colson," https://en.wikipedia.org/wiki/Charles_Colson, page 7.

Chapter 8: A Popular Movie Star

1) *Bullitt* (Warner Brothers - Seven Arts, October 1968).

2) Marc Eliot, *Steve McQueen: A Biography* (New York: Three Rivers Press, 2011), page 1.

3) Eliot, page 30.

4) Grady Ragsdale, Jr., *Steve McQueen: The Final Chapter* (Ventura, CA: Vision House, 1983) page 45. There are several secular biographies of Steve McQueen. They hardly mention his Christian conversion. The only book that goes into it in detail, other than the one by Ragsdale, is by Pastor Greg Laurie, written together with Marshall Terrill. It is titled, *Steve McQueen: The Salvation of an American Icon* (Grand Rapids, MI: Zondervan, 2019).

5) Ragsdale, page 45.

6) Ibid.

7) Ibid., page 46.

8) Ibid., page 172.

9) Ibid., pge 78.

Chapter 9: A Fortune 500 Executive

1) Mike Gendron, *Preparing for Eternity* (Proclaiming The Gospel; Third edition, 2011).

2) Mike Gendron, Contending for the Gospel (Mannart Publishers, 2019).

3) Mike Gendron's ministry, Proclaiming the Gospel, can be found on the Internet at www.Proclaiming theGospel.org.

Chapter 10: An Alcoholic

No references, except Scriptures.

Chapter 11: A Traumatized Child

No references, except Scriptures.

Chapter 12: A Drug Addict

No references, except Scriptures.

Chapter 13: A Rock Musician

No references, except Scriptures.

Chapter 14: A Scam Artist

No references, except Scriptures.

Chapter 15: A Homosexual

1) For detailed information about the two Tabernacles, see: David R. Reagan, "Worship in Bible Prophecy: The Restoration of the Tabernacle of David," https://christinprophecy.org/articles/worship-in- prophecy.

2) Mary Jones, "Randall Bane (1941-2021)." chrome-extension://efaidnbmnnnibpcajpcglclefindmkaj/https://icdf.com/sites/default/files/icdf_newsflash_special_edition.pdf, page 2.

3) Ibid., page 1.

Chapter 16: A 1960s Rebel

1) The child's diagnosis was neurofibromatosis, a genetic condition for which there is no cure. It causes tumors to grow in various parts of the body. Evelyn has written a book about her son's life and death. It is titled, *My Son, My Son: Anti-depressants, Suicide, Comfort* (2014).

2) Corrie ten Boom with C. C. Carlson, *In My Father's House: The Years before "The Hiding Place"* (Ada, MI: Fleming H. Revell Co., 1976).

3) Corrie ten Boom with John and Elizabeth Sherrill, *The Hiding Place* (Ada, MI: Chosen Books, 1971).

4) *The Hiding Place* (Burbank, CA: World Wide Pictures, 1975).

5) Evelyn has written a detailed book about her life. It is titled, *Weaving: A Journey to Corrie ten Boom Live* (Dallas, TX: Cornerstone Leadership Institute, 2007). She can be contacted through her website at https://evelynhinds.com.

Chapter 17: A Jewish Musician

1) Marty Goetz's website can be found on the Internet at https://www.martygoetz.com.

2) Marty Goetz, "A Jew Born Anew," https://www.invubu.com/music/show/song/Marty-Goetz/A-Jew-Born-Anew.html.

3) Ibid.

4) An outstanding video interview with Marty Goetz can be found on the Internet at https://ifoundshalom.com/marty-goetz.

Chapter 18: A Former Nun

1) Francis Thompson, "The Hound of Heaven," http://www.houndofheaven.com/poem.

2) William Backus and Marie Chapian, *Telling Yourself the Truth* (Bloomington, MN: Bethany House Publishers, 2014).

3) John Walvoord, *Armageddon, Oil and the Middle East Crisis* (Grand Rapids, MI: Zondervan, 1991).

Chapter 19: A Scientist

1) Excellent materials supporting Creation Science have been produced by The Institute for Creation Research (https://www.icr.org) and Answers in Genesis (https://answersingenesis.org). These materials range from pre-school all the way to the graduate level.

2) For detailed information about the history of the Messianic Jewish Movement in the United States, see: Dr. David R. Reagan, "Messianic Judaism: Its Meaning and Significance," *Lamplighter* magazine. November-December 2007, pages 3-10.

3) Richard Rogers and Oscar Hammerstein II, "South Pacific," 1949.

Lyric from the song, "Some Enchanted Evening," https://rodgers andhammerstein.com/song/south-pacific/some-enchanted-evening.

Chapter 20: A Cult Member

1) J. F. Rutherford, *Vindication*, vol. 1 (1931), www.scribd.com/docu ment/300100330/Watchtower-Vindication-Book-One-by-J-F-Ruth erford-1931.

2) Jean Eason, *A Jehovah's Witness Finds the Truth* (Love Agape Ministries Press; Revised edition 1999). This book can be downloaded free of charge from Jean Eason's website, Tutors for Christ, at https://www.tutorsforchristministry.org/history.

3) Jean Eason and Orpah Hicks, *Bird's-Eye View of the Bible* (Lexington, KY: Tutors for Christ, 2010).

Chapter 21: A Homeless Wino

1) Lamb & Lion Ministries has produced a DVD album titled, "The Life and Songs of Jack Hollingsworth. It contains six songs by Jack that have been creatively edited by the Lamb & Lion video staff plus a tribute by Dr. David Reagan to Jack's life and ministry. To order, go to https://lamblionresources.com/purchase/the-life-and-songs-of-jack -hollingsworth.

Chapter 22: A Cultural Christian

1) For a detailed presentation of Dr. Reagan's transition from an academic career into full time ministry, see his book, *Trusting God: Learning to Walk by Faith*. Originally published in 1987, it is now in its third edition (2015). This book focuses on spiritual principles for joyful, triumphal living in Christ, which Dr. Reagan learned the hard way, through experience.

Chapter 23: A Summary

1) Skip Heitzig, from a sermon heard over the Internet, https://cal varynm.church.

2) Mike Gendron, "Epochs of Time Reveal God's Wrath on Sin." www. proclaimingthegospel.org/blog/ptg-blog/epochs-of-time-display-go d-s-wrath.